More praise for

YOUTH TO POWER

"Among the many lessons in Jamie Margolin's inspiring manifesto *Youth to Power* is the counsel to 'find your why.' It is the advice of a wise elder in the voice of a young activist. Everyone, young and old, should read this enlightened and engaging call to action. It is a road map for a new generation of social activists and perhaps a critical piece of what may save us as a species and a planet. History will remember this book."

—Ken Burns

"We're at a moment when so many young people want to join in the fight for the future, but too often they feel powerless. Jamie Margolin and her many accomplices provide the sockets to plug into—the (clean) electricity comes pouring through these pages, and anyone who reads them will know what to do to make a real difference."

—Bill McKibben, founder of 350.org and
New York Times bestselling author of *Falter:
Has the Human Game Begun to Play Itself Out?*

"Jamie Margolin has been on the front lines in the fight to avert climate catastrophe. Whether young or old, please read her account, *Youth to Power*, and be inspired to join the battle."

—Michael E. Mann, co-author of *The
Madhouse Effect: How Climate Change Denial
Is Threatening Our Planet, Destroying Our
Politics, and Driving Us Crazy*

YOUTH TO POWER

Julie,

You can change the world.

Jamie Margolin

YOUTH TO POWER

YOUR VOICE
AND HOW TO USE IT

JAMIE MARGOLIN

Go
hachette
BOOKS
NEW YORK

Interviews edited for length and clarity. To read full interviews please visit
YouthToPowerBook.com.

Some names and identifying details have been changed.

Hachette Go, an imprint of Hachette Books
Hachette Book Group
1290 Avenue of the Americas
New York, NY 10104
HachetteGo.com
Facebook.com/HachetteGo
Instagram.com/HachetteGo

First Edition: June 2020

Hachette Books is a division of Hachette Book Group, Inc.

The Hachette Go and Hachette Books name and logos are trademarks of Hachette
Book Group, Inc.

The publisher is not responsible for websites (or their content) that are not owned by
the publisher.

The Hachette Speakers Bureau provides a wide range of authors for speaking events.
To find out more, go to www.hachettespeakersbureau.com or call (866) 376-6591.

Library of Congress Cataloging-in-Publication Data

Names: Margolin, Jamie, 2001- author.
Title: Youth to power : your voice and how to use it / Jamie Margolin.
Description: First edition. | New York : Hachette GO, [2020] | Includes
    bibliographical references and index. | Audience: Grades 10-12 |
    Identifiers: LCCN 2019056403 | ISBN 9780738246666 (trade paperback) |
    ISBN 9780738246673 (ebook)
Subjects: LCSH: Youth—Political activity—Juvenile literature. | Youth—
    Government policy—Juvenile literature. | Social action—Juvenile literature.
Classification: LCC HQ799.2.P6 M362 2020 | DDC 320.0835—dc23
LC record available at https://lccn.loc.gov/2019056403

ISBNs: 978-0-738-24666-6 (paperback), 978-0-738-24667-3 (ebook)

Printed in the United States of America

LSC-C

Printing 3, 2021

TO THE QUEER KIDS.
WE ARE UNSTOPPABLE.

CONTENTS

Contents

FOREWORD

THIS BOOK IS YOUR TOOLBOX
BY GRETA THUNBERG

The first time I heard of Jamie Margolin was in May 2018. We were a group of young people who were trying to organize a Zero Hour march in Sweden for the international day of action on July 21. It was just a few weeks before I started school striking outside the Swedish parliament.

Before that I basically hadn't met any young person who seemed to care about the climate, the environment, or our future survival on this planet. My idea of the youth today was that we were lazy, self-centered, and didn't spare the climate and ecological crisis even a second of our thoughts. I remember feeling so alone, it seemed as if no one my age saw what was going on around us or even wanted to make a difference—apart from people like Jamie Margolin.

Since then, I have been proven wrong over and over again. It turned out that countless young people felt just like I did. That our generation wanted to not only change the world but also save it. We just didn't know how. We didn't know how to turn our frustration and despair into something that could help push us in the right direction. And that, I think, is what's holding us back from taking action and stepping out of our comfort zones.

The more people I meet, the more I travel and get to experience, the more convinced I am that the solution to the climate and ecological crisis—as well as to many other crises—is simple: it is the people.

Above all, the young people. The power we hold within us is invincible. It is we who together are going to solve this. What we need to do now is to figure out a way to channel that power and that strength into action.

I think that tipping point we are all waiting for will happen when we the youth truly realize what we together can accomplish. I know we will pass that point sooner or later, and deep down you probably know it too. The question is just *when* that tipping point will come and whether it will come in time.

Since Zero Hour started, things have begun to move. But not nearly enough. And somehow it seems like we still are stuck. So right now we are in desperate need of guidance and something that tells us what the next—or sometimes even the first—steps are and how to take them. That is why we need books like this one.

We need to be given the tools with which we can change the world. And in this book, you can find them.

Greta Thunberg
November 12, 2019

Greta Thunberg was born in 2003. In August 2018 she started a school strike that became a movement called Fridays for Future, which has inspired school strikes for climate action in more than 150 countries, involving millions of students. Thunberg has spoken at climate rallies across Europe and at the United Nations COP24 in Poland and the World Economic Forum in Davos. In September 2019 she spoke in New York City at the UN Climate Action Summit. She has won the prestigious Prix Liberté and been nominated for a Nobel Peace Prize.

INTRODUCTION

THE WORLD NEEDS TO HEAR YOUR VOICE

In times of darkness, what has saved people, countries, and movements has been ordinary folks having the courage to speak truth to power.

But our world doesn't exactly encourage dissent.

From the minute we are tossed into preschool we are told, *Be quiet, raise your hand if you want to speak, listen to authority always, put your head down and do your work, and never question anything you are told. Memorize information and regurgitate it back onto a piece of paper.* We are told, *If you follow the rules, there is a safe and clear path ahead of you: get good grades and you'll be successful. Study hard for a bright future.*

But what happens when there is no future to study for? What happens when, for example, your generation is being left with a planet that is soon going to be unable to sustain human civilization because of climate change?

Then the cookie-cutter rules we are supposed to follow no longer apply. That safe and clear path of following the steps of the school system into a bright and successful future no longer works in a climate-change-warped world where we are guaranteed no tomorrow.

And unfortunately, all that memorizing, studying, and rule following we got so good at won't help us save ourselves. The longer you live in a world that sees you as just another cog in the machine, the more your eyes glaze over the injustices in front of you—and the less you question.

Many adults in today's society (not all of them though, and shout-out to the indigenous elders who have been fighting the good fight long before I was born) have pretty much lost their will to question and rebel, or their energy is drained from doing so their entire life. Don't get me wrong, our elders have lots of wisdom and experience to share with us, and to make changes in the world, our movements must be intergenerational. We cannot pit generations against each other or forget the decades of hard changemaking work that came before us. Erasing the work of our ancestors is extremely disrespectful and harmful to our own work because we are shutting ourselves off from knowledge of the past. We the youth are standing on the shoulders of the changemakers before us, and we must always acknowledge and respect that. Still, a lot of the action adults in power are currently taking to combat the biggest issues our generation is facing, like climate change, operates according to the same oppressive logic and methods that created the issues in the first place.

But young people? We are yet to be broken and burned out. We are still closer than adults to that part of ourselves that is full of questions, challenges, and a refusal to accept the state of the world around us. We have fresh energy, insight, and a unique power to create change in our world. What we get in trouble most for at school is usually questioning the rules. But questioning the rules may actually be where our greatest power lies.

People often joke that young people are always on the right side of history, but I believe it is a full truth, not just a witty joke. History has proved that we are always on the right side of history over and over again.

Who helped Martin Luther King Jr. win crucial civil rights battles while he was in jail and beginning to lose hope? Youth. The Children's March in Birmingham, Alabama, in the 1960s changed the game in the civil rights movement and led to the end of segregation.

Who started the revolutionary #NODAPL movement to try to stop the Dakota Access Pipeline? Youth. The indigenous youth of the Standing Rock Sioux reservation went against the orders of their elders and started a movement that forever changed how we fight the fossil fuel industry and united Native communities like never before.

The voices of young people are so powerful because we have the moral high ground on pretty much every issue you can name.

We didn't create any of the systems of oppression that hold us and our world down; they were thrust upon us at birth whether we liked it or not. We have no hidden agenda.

Youth have nothing selfish to gain from our activism. There is hardly ever any monetary reward for being an activist, and any fame that comes along with it is rare and usually meager and fleeting.

Youth don't speak out of a corrupt motive. We speak truth to power because we genuinely want change and to create a better world. And this is why the voices of youth are so pure and powerful, why they always have been, and why they always will be.

Young people, despite our society conditioning us to follow the rules blindly, still have that knack for seeing right through the BS we are fed. The youth right now are the truth right now—and it's always been that way. Whether the adults who run our society admit to it or not.

My name is Jamie, as of this writing I'm in high school, and there is absolutely nothing special about me. I wasn't born into a political family, an activist family, or a rich family. No one held my hand and walked me through the changemaking process. I was (and still am) just a girl trying to survive high school without losing my mind, who also happens to be fed up with the corruption and irresponsibility of leaders and the crumbling unlivable world my generation is being left with.

This is the book I desperately wished I had when I was fourteen and just starting my activism journey, with no clue of what I was getting into. Every word within these pages is the true, unfiltered advice and experiences of a young activist who wants to make sure other youth activists have a guide to doing this work from someone in the same situation who actually knows what it's like.

Within these pages you'll find my inside scoop on movement building, community organizing, nonprofits, and making change. This is a guide to being a young changemaker. The world of changemaking can be thrilling and empowering, and it can give you a sense of hope and relief in the face of the challenges you're up against.

I have spoken to many amazing young people with so much to say and so much to offer the world who were convinced that they were not good enough. These incredible activists (whose conversations made me change the way I worked and functioned for the better) were still convinced they weren't smart enough, brave enough, or whatever enough to be changemakers.

Whoever told you that you don't belong in the political world or that you do not have what it takes to fight for a cause is full of it. You (Yes, YOU!) belong with us, the young people changing the world.

Introduction

You are one of us. Welcome.

This journey of being an activist is something I would not trade for anything else in the world. Wherever you are in your journey is okay—whether you're still a bit nervous about dipping your toe into the tumultuous waters of making an impact, or whether you are confident and ready to go but just need the right guidance to move forward. If lobbying your elected officials is scary to you, if you're nervous about getting into protests and community organizing, that's totally okay! Just because you are uncomfortable speaking up now doesn't mean you'll never get there. In your activism journey you will find allies along the way; you will grow and learn and evolve, and wherever it is you want to be, you will get there, I promise. I know because not very long ago I was you. I was an insecure fourteen-year-old, worried and scared about the state of the world, with no clue how to get started.

Just like I wish someone would have done for me when I began my activism, I will keep it real and tell you everything. The good and the bad. What to watch out for, problems I dealt with (so you know how to navigate them!), and all of that tough stuff that tends to get brushed over with flowery font and inspirational blanket statements.

As a chronically exhausted high school student with too much homework who's running an international movement, I don't have time to sugarcoat. What you get in this book, on top of advice and strategies, are my real stories about life as a youth activist: from joyfully protesting outside the Supreme Court in a bitter cold torrential rainstorm, to a fossil fuel lobbyist creepily grabbing my shoulder and calling me "sweetie," to dealing with all the challenges of the internal workings of a large organization. I've also placed excerpts of interviews with other young activists who inspire me at the end of every chapter so you can get other perspectives on the diversity of social justice work out there. You can read the full interviews on-line at YouthToPowerBook.com. My hope is that these stories help guide you, inspire you, give you courage—and in some cases serve as a perfect example of what *not* to do.

My reality and that of all changemakers isn't a montage of flashy protest footage set to dramatic music. The pictures you see on social media of majestic-looking young people marching tri-umphantly are not even close to the full story. Most of my life (and the lives of all the youth activists I know and work with) consists of trying to get through my inbox while juggling homework and extracurriculars, and taking back-to-back video conference calls during breaks in my school's badly lit costume closet. It makes the video of me look like I have four chins no matter what angle I try.

This book is your guide to causing good trouble, unlearning everything you've been taught before, disrupting the status quo, making your voice heard, challenging problematic authority, changing the culture, changing laws, and yes, changing the world.

This is the manifesto of the youth revolution.

Dog-ear it, write in it, read it out of order, highlight what you want, rip out pages and tape them to your bedroom wall, flush it down the toilet if that's what helps you process information better—I won't be offended (or maybe don't; that would clog your toilet).

I am in the same boat as you, and I'm not going to order you around and act like I'm better than you or pretend to know ev-erything. The truth is, I am still learning, just like you. We're in this together.

This is your guide to starting your own revolution, whatever that means to you.

Join me.

Keep reading, and we can be scrappy activists together.

Scrappy activists who *win*.

Jamie Margolin, Eighteen, She/Her
Founder of Zero Hour, plaintiff with Our Children's
Trust, climate justice activist, writer, advocate for
LGBTQ+ youth and queer women

I was in second grade when I first tried to take climate action. I grew up watching documentaries about the climate crisis and environmental destruction, which filled me with fear and dread for my future. I wanted to act, but I didn't know how. I made little Green Club pins and handed them out to students, telling them, "Join me if you care about saving the earth."

The world kept sending me the message that I had to wait until I was older and graduated college to have an impact on the world, so I talked to my friends and did school projects, and that was the extent of my activism. It didn't feel like enough. It was during the 2016 election when I realized I held special power and knowledge as a young person and I finally had enough of staying quiet.

In my freshman year of high school, I was the youngest intern at my local campaign office. After the election season was over, I joined grassroots groups in my community doing the crucial but unglamorous work of educating and lobbying elected officials and my community about the climate crisis and demanding commonsense action.

I didn't believe the adults in the room respected my voice as a young person, so I took my activism to the national level, founding Zero Hour: an international youth climate justice organization. Zero Hour led the official Youth Climate March in Washington, DC, and in more than twenty-five sister cities all around the world during the summer of 2018. My organization laid the groundwork for and inspired the current school strike for climate movement. As the youth climate movement rises in profile, I stay grounded in addressing the root systems of oppression, like colonialism, that caused the climate crisis in the first place.

Along this crazy journey I also became a plaintiff in Our Children's Trust's Youth versus the government of Washington State lawsuit called *Aji P. v. State of Washington*, suing my home state of Washington for denying my generation's constitutional right to a livable environment. Today I continue to organize and mobilize for climate justice, and I give speeches around the world educating and rallying people for the cause. By making mistakes, trying, failing, working my butt off, and learning from others, I have learned the ropes of being an organizer and activist, and I'm dishing everything I know so you don't have to dig for the knowledge yourself. Instead of making you go fishing like I had to starting out, my hope is that this book will make your changemaking journey a lot more accessible.

FINDING YOUR *WHY*

FINDING YOUR *WHY* IS THE FIRST STEP ON YOUR ACTIVISM JOURNEY.

The first and most important step to being an activist is to find your *why*.

Before we get into any specifics of how one goes about community organizing and movement building, this is the foundational step of your changemaking journey: making it clear to yourself why you are an activist and what exactly it is you are fighting for.

It is critical to ground yourself in what you're fighting for before jumping in headfirst and to continue keeping yourself grounded throughout the whole journey. Having a clear reason and intention for what you are doing helps lead you in the right direction. There are so many organizations, causes, groups, and methods to create change, it can be hard to choose a path if you don't have a strong grounding reason why.

Why is not a specific goal—it's the core driving reason for you to be doing what you are doing. Your *why* is something that will likely never change; it is what you are fighting for that you cannot live without.

It's not your short-term goals or even your long-term goals. Your *why* is not media attention or even organizing a protest, stopping a pipeline, or any specific goal or target, because those change. Let's say you defeat the pipeline. You stage the protest. You get tons of media for your activism—what happens then?

Every activist has a *why*. Think about it this way—every protest you attend, every event you organize, every article you write, every job you take or don't take are all just strategies to get to and serve your *why*. They are not the end goals in themselves. Every campaign you take on, conference you attend, and speech you give—they are all tiny steps, tiny puzzle pieces, part of the strategy to get to your *why* and serve it.

Every single action you take going forward needs to serve your *why*. That's how you're going to be successful. That's how you're going to stick with it in the long run and make that change you have been striving for.

My *why* is the cause that when I turn off all distractions, all external feedback, all noise and really just live with myself for a moment always stays the same. It is protecting the Pacific Northwest, where I grew up.

If there's one lesson for you to take away from this entire book it's that every tip and trick about movement building and organizing is going to be a waste of your time unless you find your *why*.

So, tell me, Why are you doing this?

Why are you an activist?

Why are you joining a movement?

Why are you starting a movement?

Why are you fighting for change?

Is it a place you love that is deeply dear to you that you cannot bear the thought of losing?

Is it someone in particular you're fighting for? A person, community, or group of people?

Is there something that happened to you or someone you love that you want to make sure never, *ever* happens to anyone again?

Is there something you live with and are going through that you need the world to understand?

Is it because someone showed you how you participated in an unjust system and you want to help others break free too? Because you or your ancestors participated in a culture of harm that you feel activated to try to repair?

Take some time alone, however long you need, and mull this over. There's no rush. Finding your *why* does *not* mean that you have to lock yourself in a room for a week and wrack your brain until you find it. It does *not* mean you are barred from attending a protest or rally or community organizing meeting until you find it. Usually, finding what makes you tick is an active process that involves self-reflection and experimentation. You can attend all sorts of events and activities and explore what you are fighting for freely, openly, and unrestrictedly. Also keep in mind that your *why* doesn't have to be something out of this world, grand, or extraordinary.

For example, for Natalie Mebane, a beloved adult mentor of mine, her *why* is a bay she loves in Trinidad and Tobago, where she spent most of her childhood. Natalie is a climate justice activist, and when I asked her, "Why are you doing this work?" she simply sent me a picture of that bay where she played with her family as a kid. It's a place beloved to her, that is part of her heritage as a Caribbean woman that she takes pride in, that is being destroyed by climate change. She would be heartbroken to live without it. Natalie always tells me, if she had all the money in the world, she would spend every second of her days in that bay in Trinidad and Tobago. It's what she is truly fighting for. It keeps her rooted no matter what her job as an organizer throws at her.

So, get to a quiet place where it's just you and your thoughts. Remove all distractions and external influences. Turn off your phone and just have a good old honest chat with yourself. Be the annoying toddler who won't stop asking *why*. When you first try to give yourself shallow, superficial answers, keep probing "why" until you can't go any deeper.

I'll share my *why* with you: why I am a climate justice activist, why I started my organization, why I'm suing my government, why I speak out is to protect the beautiful Pacific Northwest. It is where I was raised, the only place I remember living, where I wrote this book, and it is in my very biased opinion the most beautiful place in the world. Although I was born in Los Angeles and my mom is an immigrant from Colombia, and although I plan to live all over the United States and maybe spend some time in my mom's home country in South America, the Pacific Northwest will forever own my heart. The mountains and hills and oceans and flora and fauna and the culture and life of Seattle is what I live for. My *why*, when you boil it down, is defending the sacred life of the Pacific Northwest. I could not live without the crisp air, the tall evergreens, the salty ocean, the birds, the salmon, the deer, the bears, the seals, the orcas, the smell of the cedars right after it rains.

I am not a religious person. The closest feeling I have to spirituality is the sacredness of the Pacific Northwest environment around me . . . and climate change is threatening all of it. The ecosystems of the ocean and all of their marvelous life are unraveling, the salmon are dying, the orcas are going extinct, I never see the seals anymore, the skies are getting more and more polluted, the forests are being destroyed, and the oceans are acidifying because of the high carbon levels that are destroying not only the sea life but also the Seattle sea-based culture.

Also keep in mind that you can have more than one *why*, and it can be different for each cause you take on.

My *why* for being an LGBTQ+ activist is rooted in my experiences as a lesbian living in a heteronormative world (a world that sees being straight as the norm). My *why*, the reason I am such a vocal advocate for my queer community, is that I have experienced shame, stress, depression, alienation, and anxiety because of the way our world treats and erases girls like me, and I am striving to create a world where I don't have to go through that anymore, and neither does anyone else. I don't want any other queer kid to feel as overwhelmingly unrepresented, unwelcome, and unwanted by society as I have felt and often still do; I want to make a world where we have achieved full equality and liberation everywhere. Slightly different from my climate activism *why*, my LGBTQ+ activism *why* is rooted in my identity and personal lived experiences. My reasons are simple and genuine, because they are rooted in the liberation and ultimately survival of an oppressed group I belong to.

So, what are YOU fighting for? What can't you live without? What is being taken from you?

Close this book, and maybe tonight before you fall asleep, just sit there and really ask yourself, "What is my *why*?"

You got it?

Good.

Hang on to it.

Make a vision board with it, draw it, write about it, make a video for yourself. Make reminders visible around you, especially where you work. Because I can tell you from experience that the movement-building road ahead of you is going to be one hell of a ride.

But you know why you're doing this, so it's going to be incredibly worth it. Buckle up and let's do this!

Juan David Giraldo Mendoza, Nineteen, He/Him, and Alejandro Lotero Cedeño, Eighteen, He/Him
Climate justice activists, Fridays for Future Colombia

JAMIE: How did you become an activist?

JUAN: The Colombian state did not want to help fund public schools, so I joined the entire university community and went on strike. Thousands of people marched in the streets. Even faculty and staff joined us. After four months of ignoring the protests, the president of Colombia finally came. Other Latin American countries sent support. It was so much pressure that the government gave the school system the funding. That's when I understood the power of the people.

Then I read a book called *The 6th Extinction,* which is about the climate crisis. I saw the original Fridays for Future video from Greta Thunberg, who was calling for a school strike for climate action. I was obsessed with the climate crisis. Soon it became too much, and I had a panic attack about climate change.

On January 15, 2019, I sat in front of the Gobernación de Antioquia and became the first person in Latin America to school strike for climate action. Soon after, Alejandro started striking in his community, and we met online and started school strikes in other parts of Colombia.

JAMIE: What have been your biggest challenges as activists?

JUAN: State violence repressing our protests. The anti-protesters here are known as ESMAD (Mobile Anti-Disturbance Squadron), and they use a lot of tactics to crack down on our demonstrations. We in Colombia technically have the right to protest, but it is not respected or protected. In Bogota, there were one hundred students in the street demonstrating, and they were chased by a truck.

The problem is that the media distorts a lot of what happens. It happened a lot with the university strikes. ESMAD would hit us and beat us up, and then they would put it on TV as if we the students were bad and ESMAD had no choice but to do their jobs. They criminalized us in the press, which gave the police more justification to attack us. In the media they do not even talk about why the protest is happening. They put the blame on us for being "violent" kids.

ALEJANDRO: In the places where I strike, the police bother us a lot. They do not like us to protest. It is an effort to get people out, and often not many people go to strikes, or listen to us and pay attention to this crisis. If I did not have a lot of emotional resilience, I could not do this work.

YOUR FIRST STEPS

TIME TO ROLL UP YOUR SLEEVES
AND DO THE WORK!

Okay, you know why you're in this changemaking world, and you're ready to get started. You're fired up and ready to go, but there's only one problem...as you're sitting there zoning out in math class you realize, *I have no clue how to get started!*

When I was fourteen years old, enraged with the world around me and ready to make a change, I had absolutely no clue where to begin. I wanted to join a political campaign, join a movement, help my community, engage my school in issues that mattered, make something, do something *big*.

I saw all these activists online leading movements, and it was so easy to get inspired...but it was hard to know how to take the first step in that direction.

Before we get into how to take your first steps as an activist, let's define what an activist is. First of all, there is no one true definition: there are many different forms of changemaking, one no more important than another.

Starting a Black student union at your school or university to provide a space for Black youth to build power together makes you an activist, just like starting a nonprofit makes you an activist.

For some people, activism looks like engaging your school. For others, it's running a blog and social media pages talking about your personal story and important issues that are often overlooked by our colonized society. For others, it's mobilizing in the streets and knocking on doors of elected officials. You don't have to choose only one way of effecting change, and you don't have to feel pressure that the first thing you try is going to be what you're stuck with.

Finding the right space for your energy is like trying on clothes. You can wear a shirt as long as you need to, and when it no longer fits, then try something new.

So when it comes to looking for that first club, organization, nonprofit, community organization, or whatever you want to do to kick off your journey, don't put too much pressure on yourself that this has to be *the* thing you do. In fact, take all the pressure off, and just be open to learning. You don't have to limit yourself to joining just one group or organization; you can be a part of many, and the form of your activism may change over the years.

Now is the time to put your feelers out, experiment, and *learn*.

It's important to remember that most of the time, the journey that completely transforms your life starts with something as small as an email.

My activism started with clicking on an ad from my local Democratic Party for a phone-banking campaign event, which prompted me to RSVP. So I did.

A single RSVP catapulted me into a career/journey/way of life that completely changed me forever.

Let me explain: For some reason, political campaigns during the 2016 presidential election had gotten hold of my email. I was getting spam from campaigns saying things like, **Bill Joe Candidate needs YOU to donate before tonight's deadline or else we will all DIE**—you know, campaign stuff.

One of the emails right before the general election season caught my eye. It said that the campaign office was looking for new volunteers to make phone calls encouraging people to register to vote. At that point I was so fed up with what I was seeing from certain candidates on TV that I decided it was time to stop yelling at the screen and time to start getting out the vote. I walked into that campaign office and gave everything I could of my time and energy to what I believed was saving democracy. Soon I went from volunteer to intern to unofficial Spanish translator of the office (being the only Latina there) to well-respected regular and volunteer trainer around the Seattle Democratic headquarters.

I'm sure after all of the introduction and hype of the previous two chapters, you're expecting some kind of master strategy. Some grand first jump and complex to-do list of how to transform into whatever your vision is of a megaphone-wielding, street-marching radical activist. But it's really this simple:

HOW TO BEGIN

1. Find an organization, political campaign, community group, or something that you want to be a part of, volunteer with, or even just learn more about.
2. Find their website, social media page, or any other platform of information where you can find an email or phone number to contact someone there.
3. Send them a message or call them, ask some questions, and tell them you'd like to get involved and a little bit about your story, who you are, and why you care, or subscribe to their newsletter to get a feel for what they do.

4. Just take the leap and join a meeting, attend an event, and take it from there.
5. Be open to learning, and learn by doing.
6. Figure out your *why*.

When I was first trying to get involved in the environmental movement, I had no clue where to start. So I googled local youth environmental organizations in my area and called one of them, Plant for the Planet Seattle (a.k.a. Climate Change for Families). My call got picked up on the first ring, and I just laid it all out: "Look, I'm fourteen, I have no clue what I'm doing, but I am really worried about climate change and I want to do something about it."

They said something along the lines of, "I can work with that," and I attended their first meeting. I sat in the back of the room, with no clue what was going on. I was surrounded by people my age or younger who had been doing this work for years, and compared to them I felt so insecure and inferior. *That twelve-year-old has done more to fight the climate crisis than I ever will be able to!*

There's nothing that makes you feel worse about yourself than being in a room of younger people you assume are way ahead of you on your activism journey. But I swallowed my insecurity and decided, *I'm going to be just like those kids. I can do it too.* So I attended more and more meetings. I began to ask questions and learn, I brought up ideas and initiatives, and Plant for the Planet Seattle gave me the space and time to grow and learn and take leadership.

All the supportive adult allies at Plant for the Planet taught me everything they knew, and they supported and guided me as I became a community organizer in the city and grew as an activist. And it wasn't just the adults who accepted me into the activist family and lifted me up. I also learned from and was quickly accepted by my fellow youth activists. The whole gang at Plant for the Planet Seattle welcomed me with open arms. We sang *Hamilton* songs at the top of our lungs on road trips to Olympia to lobby for climate bills, ate pancakes together after uncomfortable interactions with those politicians, and talked politics for hours on end. I found a community and became the activist I wanted to be simply because I googled an organization, called the number, and took the plunge.

There is no amount of research and preparation you can do before getting involved that will fully prepare you to be an organizer. The only way to learn is by just starting. Join that organization, perform whatever tasks they give you, and have an open mind. Talk to people, observe, and ask questions.

You should also accept early on that you're going to make mistakes. As a perfectionist, I don't like the idea of having a 100 percent chance that I am going to mess up over and over again and that I will never fully know it all—but that's the deal in this field. You just have to keep questioning, educating yourself, and doing. Don't sit on your computer frantically researching. Take a step out the door, assist a local organization in whatever they need, and let the ultimate teacher—trial and error—take the lead.

OTHER WAYS TO START MAKING CHANGES THAT AREN'T NECESSARILY COMMUNITY/NONPROFIT RELATED

1. Write a letter or email (or call!) to your elected official (especially local): It's actually very easy to get in contact with your representative.

    Deeply upset with the outcome of an election that I had poured my heart and soul into, I didn't know where to turn. I wanted to make sure that my voice and concerns were heard by my politicians currently in office. So I got out my computer and started drafting letters to members of my local state legislature, like different state senators, my mayor, and members of the Seattle City Council. Keep in mind that I had never written to an elected official before. I was just a freshman in high school without any idea of how to contact politicians.

Writing or calling your elected officials can be a really great way to start voicing your opinions and concerns to those in power, and it is accessible from wherever you are. Before I found my home in the community organizing/nonprofit world, I would call or write my state legislators about my concern about the climate crisis a few times a week. The letters I wrote were not formal or worded in an inauthentic style. You don't have to go above and beyond to write the fanciest letter known to mankind. Just speak from the heart, talk the way you normally express yourself while being polite and professional, and send it.

It only takes a quick Google search to find the district you live in at different levels of government (state, municipal, federal) and just a little more clicking around to find an email, mailing address, and phone number of representatives at each level. Keep in mind that when you are contacting a politician, the person on the other end of the line is usually their assistant of some sort or a legislative aide—but they are the ones who often help craft the policy that the politician votes on, so it's important to make connections with them as well.

If you really want the elected official to personally see your message, you can ask the aide to pass the message along to their boss. Your voice deserves to be heard in the political system, even if you are too young to vote, and you can contact an elected official from just about anywhere. There are different ways change can be made—some involve breaking the rules of the system, others involve playing by the rules. Both are valuable, and if you're not ready to break any rules just yet, this method of making those in power listen can be very effective.

Here is a sample email I wrote to my local elected officials, to show you how simple it is! Make sure that you contact only your own representatives, because politicians tend to mostly care about messages coming from their own district. Why? Because they are only responsible to represent the people who elected them, the members of their own districts. So if an elected official receives a message from someone outside of their constituency, it's not going to be received with much urgency. (Email usually only works with really local politicians, like state senators and state representatives who actually read their emails. With senators and other higher officeholders, letter writing and phone calls have been proven most effective. I sent the below email to my state representative soon after President Trump was elected in the United States. I was terrified of what was to come.) Take a look:

SUBJECT: 15-year-old girl concerned about freedom of speech and press

MESSAGE:

I'm a 15-year-old girl and political writer for the *Huffington Post* and *Seattle Times,* and a member of my school's Junior Statesmen of America team.

I'm very concerned about the "post-truth" era of Donald Trump and how opinions are becoming facts and vice versa.

Donald Trump has shown many signs of an autocrat, and I am becoming more scared every day that this war on the media, disregard for facts, and attacking of everyone who criticizes him is going to seep into our foundations and permanently damage our democracy and what our country stands for. I'm really scared the US is going to turn into something like Putin's Russia. What can be done?

THE REPRESENTATIVE'S RESPONSE (verbatim):

Thank you for writing, Jamie. One reason I am hopeful that our country and the world will be able to survive Donald Trump is because young people like yourself see Trump and everything he represents far more clearly than people four times your age.

It is important that we continue to call out every instance we see of the erosion of our democracy, whether that is Trump/Republicans attacking democratic institutions, intimidation of the press, or normalization of corruption. We cannot grow numb to these things and we must continue to call them out.

I am also encouraged that Trump is starting his presidency with far lower approval ratings than any president in history, so while there is much work to be done to turn things around, at least most Americans already see Trump as the fraud that he is.

Please continue to stay aware and make others aware of the threat Trump poses to American democracy. We must continue to call out violations for the next four years, at which time you and many others your age will be eligible to vote and to turn things around for our country and our world (as clearly the United States is not the only country that has seen the deterioration of democratic norms lately—Turkey, the Philippines, and Poland are all other worrisome examples).

It's as easy as that! Your letter or call to your representative can be as long or short as you need it to be—you are getting the message out there!

2. **Join a protest/demonstration or drop by a campaign office during a campaign season:** You can bypass the whole step of calling and contacting: just show up to any kind of public activism event to participate. If there is a march or strike or any sort of public action, you can just slip in and join. Get a feel for it, and if you like what you see and what you did, find the organizers of that event and ask them how you can get more involved with similar actions.

3. **Start posting on social media about the issues you care about and personal stories that intertwine with that:** You don't have to wait until you've been working for a nonprofit for two years to start using social media and blogging platforms to share the stories and issues you care about. There is no set requirement for when you can start opening up about something that has been hurting you or bothering you. I have a friend who uses her Instagram to post about what it's like to live with a chronic illness that has rendered her disabled, and that is her way of starting the conversation about disability rights, raising awareness about youth with chronic illnesses and disabilities, and amplifying their voices. She is working on starting a YouTube channel, filming videos in her room about topics surrounding being young and disabled that are neglected by mainstream media. So go ahead and start right now. Write that post and film that video about something you've gone through that you've been dying to tell. Gathering

the courage to finally publicly share your story can be that moment of stepping into the activist realm.

4. **Start with a school project or a neighborhood initiative:** Start engaging your own school and neighborhood. Are there problems plaguing your school that no one has taken it upon themselves to fix? Gather a group of people, and work on fixing them yourself! Is there a club at your school or university or an organization in your neighborhood like a multicultural student union, environmental club, or queer-straight alliance that doesn't exist but should? Create that club! Is there a problem young people in your community are struggling with, like mental health or police brutality? Start a support group. Could your campus be more environmentally conscious or better allies to certain groups of people? Gather a group of people to start working on bettering your community.

Improving your school, community, or neighborhood may seem small-time, but I am dead serious when I say almost all real change starts from the bottom up, directly impacting a few people most successfully. That success allows the effort to expand in scale. If you're a student, going to school is like a full-time job. So why not improve the conditions or make an impact in the place you spend most of your days? The same goes for working any kind of job outside of school. Do working conditions need to be improved? Start there.

I should also point out that it is important in this process for you to start thinking about where you get your power and growing into your power.

Yes, I said growing into your power because you already have power. As a young person, your power comes from your unique set of lived experiences and perspectives that the world needs to hear. You just need to tap into it. What makes your voice worth listening to on the topic you're tackling? Do you have a personal story of struggling with the issue? Does it affect your family or community? That authority on a topic gives you power and will propel you forward in your work.

For example, if you want to get involved with a Hispanic immigration rights organization because you or your family are immigrants from a Latin American country, that is power in itself. You are the one who knows your own story. You know how you've been affected, so you know what kind of solutions you and your community need. Your own lived experiences are just as valuable in your work as an activist as any PhD on that subject. Think of your own story of adversity (if you've faced any) and why your voice is powerful.

Like I said before, my big leap into the world of activism was clicking an RSVP on an ad for phone banking. I've always been the kind of person who questions norms. Ever since I can remember, I've always been hyper-political. (I mean, I grew up watching political satire like *The Colbert Report* and *The Daily Show* even when I technically wasn't allowed to.)

I'll never forget the first day I walked into my local Democratic Party campaign office. It was the July before the 2016 election, and after the Democratic Convention on TV, I was fired up to volunteer for my local party's campaigns. The campaign office was packed, and staff members quickly ushered me into a crowded room where, squished between what seemed like a million other volunteers, I got a quick orientation and was handed a call script with talking points. After practicing a few times with the staffers, I picked up one of the phones they gave us at the office (so strangers wouldn't have my personal information), and I made my very first political phone call, and then another, and then another. The first few were nerve wracking. I stuck to the script verbatim, terrified to talk to strangers. But then it got easier.

The next week, I was back to knock on doors. The week after that, I made some more phone calls. And then I couldn't wait a week anymore: I was back only a few days later, ready to knock on doors again. I became a regular at the campaign office. All the staffers learned my name and started to give me more and more responsibility. Soon, I signed on as an intern for one of the field organizers (people who work on organizing and mobilizing their local community to vote, going out into the "field"—a.k.a. the community—to make grassroots connections for a campaign), and I progressively began spending more time at my state's Democratic headquarters. The office became my home away from home. When I had a day off school, I went to the campaign office and worked a full seven hours. On weekends, I turned down my friends' invitations to hang out and worked at the campaign office. After school, I was at the campaign office.

I worked my butt off canvassing, training volunteers, making phone calls (taking the verbal abuse of grumpy old guys who weren't very happy to get campaign calls), organizing, handling an out-of-state voter intimidation case over the phone (as they needed a Spanish translator), painstakingly entering data into the computer system, and publishing an op-ed about the election in my local newspaper.

Now you may be thinking, *This sounds great and all, but Jamie, I can't see myself publishing an op-ed, knocking on doors, or putting up with grumpy old men yelling at me over the phone!* Look, I get it. You don't have to do those things. That's just what I ended up doing. It may seem, on the page, like a progression of events that happened naturally. Like I just tripped into a campaign office, and suddenly I was a successful activist doing everything I set out to do. But it didn't happen like that. Throughout my whole time at the campaign office, I was stumbling along, learning as I went, and dealing with the situations (and opportunities) given to me because I stuck around and did the hard work.

Amazing things began to happen. Major politicians made surprise appearances at the office: senators, my governor, even the presidential nominee herself, Hillary Clinton.

I was able to volunteer at a town hall and was even the first at the event to ask a question about an issue I cared about—in front of an audience of about seven hundred people.

You see what I mean about learning by doing? You just have to show up, make it clear you're open to taking on tasks and are ready to learn, and then gradually prove yourself and ask for more, make more connections, learn more…it snowballs. But no snowballing is going to happen unless you open that door, make yourself available, and just dive in and *do*.

Even though the 2016 election did not turn out the way I had worked so hard for it to go, being an intern at the campaign office transformed my life for the better. It opened the door to the world of civic and political engagement. And now that the door was open, I could never go back. I had finally gotten a taste of what it's like to be a part of something bigger than myself. After all those years of watching the news, political commentary, and caring about the world around me but feeling so helpless, like I was sitting on my hands with nothing to do, I had finally channeled my energy into making a difference. The feeling was intoxicating and thrilling. I had to get more!

It's time for you to get that taste as well. What are you waiting for? Go send that email! Make that call! Attend that event! Put this book down and make it happen.

I'm waiting…once you've reached out and taken that first step, flip the page and let's keep going.

Pidgeon Pagonis, Thirty-Three, They/Them
Intersex Justice Project organizer,
LGBTQ+ rights activist

JAMIE: You started out as a youth activist, and I want readers to understand they can continue to make change for the rest of their lives. So let's start at the beginning: When and how did you come out as intersex and then found your organization?

PIDGEON: It all began when the first intersex person I had met and become close to spoke on *Oprah* and I was in the audience. I realized then that you can tell your story and be honest, and people will still respect you.

Since the 1950s this bodily mutilation of intersex children has been going on, but the resistance didn't begin until the 1990s, when those kids had grown up and found the truth. That was when people started standing up and saying doctors shouldn't have the right to destroy our bodies just to make us "normal."

For my college thesis I invited my family, and I said, "I'm intersex, this is my story, and here are the stories of others." And that was the first time I told it.

I cofounded the Intersex Justice Project. We protest hospitals and surgeons that are doing cosmetic surgeries on kids too young to know what is happening to them, who don't have the ability to consent.

JAMIE: What are your tips for young LGBTQ+ and activists of other marginalized identities fighting for respect of their existence?

PIDGEON: Share the workload, share the burden. The best work happens when you're doing it in solidarity with community. Most people just see the protest, but the actual community building comes when you're sharing food, painting signs, and strategizing together. So even if the police shut your protest down, that's okay, because you've already done work building solidarity and community.

Learn how to adjust expectations and set tiny goalposts for you and your organizing work. It's important not to only think that the BIG goal is the only thing that matters. Part of pacing yourself and enjoying the changemaking process is learning how to celebrate "wins."

Also to stay sane as an activist, it's important to have variety in your life. There have been times when being an "intersex rights activist" has taken over my whole identity. If we make something our one hundred percent, we are going to burn out.

Remember that you are more than just your job, the movement, your cause. You are also a sibling, daughter, friend, lover, pet lover, artist, writer, whatever it is that makes you, YOU. Don't let go of those other crucial parts of yourself. Without taking care of yourself, you will not be able to be your best self for the movement.

POLITICAL WRITING AND PUBLISHING TO GET A MESSAGE ACROSS

USING THE KEYBOARD IN FRONT OF YOU TO MAKE YOUR VOICE HEARD.

Start with what you have. Maybe you don't have a knack for public speaking, maybe you're not ready to visit a politician's office and let them know how you feel, maybe working in a group setting is really uncomfortable for you and you just need some time to grow as an activist and process alone, while still making the change you want to see in the world.

That is why writing exists. As a writer myself, I like to think of writing as saying something important to the world without actually having to interact face to face with humans, because sometimes human interaction is to be avoided for us introverts. Using your voice as a writer can be the most accessible way of getting your story out into the world. If you have a disability or chronic health issue that changes the parameters of your mobility or other aspects of your life, if you live in an area that isn't safe to protest, if you are shy or an introvert or still just a bit uncomfortable with the idea of talking to and working with people all the time in order to get the work you want done, writing can help you make an impact. Now, I realize not all of you reading this are introverts, and the truth is, political writing and editorials are great message- and awareness-spreading tools for every activist to have in their arsenal, regardless of how much you work with others face to face. Writing can be the bulk of your activism, a fairly large part of it, a small part of it, or just a strategy for spreading the word when necessary.

For me, writing was my very first form of activism even before I RSVP'd to that campaign event back when I was fourteen. Even when I was thirteen, I wrote essays, blog posts, op-eds, and editorials about issues I cared about, things I was going through, stories of my background and my passions. I posted them on a teen blogging platform called Teen Ink, and it was my first experience writing about issues that were important to me in a public forum. It was a way to express myself and make my voice heard when I didn't have any other outlet.

Being a young person means that your political writing offers the world something special. Oftentimes, our voices are not heard on the news, and many of us are under voting age, so our needs are not heard through the political system. Youth perspectives are extremely important to hear because there are issues that deeply affect us that we need our leaders to take action on *now* (like climate change!) but our generation doesn't have a say in.

Political writing with op-eds and letters to the editor can help bridge that gap and force older people to take our necessities seriously. Because the vast majority of voters who turn out to the polls are senior citizens and middle-aged adults, the political system has catered to their opinions and needs. According to the US Census Bureau, in 2018, among those aged sixty-five and older, voter turnout was 65 percent for women and 68 percent for men. In contrast, 38 percent of women eighteen to twenty-nine years old voted, and 33 percent of men of that age group voted. And this is not a one-time thing; for decades, older folks have voted in vastly larger numbers than youth. (Which is something we *must* change by the way! Hey, youth eligible to vote—VOTE!)

Don't get me wrong; older people's needs should be met by the political system—the problem comes when their voices are the *only* ones paid attention to, leaving politicians and the media blind to what millions of young people are going through. It's crucial for the world to hear your voice. And if you have access to a computer you can type on and the internet, you have everything you need to make a big impact.

So let's get into it. What are op-eds and letters to the editor, and how do you write and publish them?

WHAT IS AN OP-ED?

An op-ed, short for "opposite the editorial page" or "opinion editorial," is a prose piece that expresses the opinion of an author usually not affiliated with the publication's editorial board. So anyone, including you, can write an op-ed for *any* newspaper or magazine! Its subject is usually a current event. There is no age restriction for who can write an op-ed! From a local newspaper to the *New York Times,* your voice could be featured, and you could help the world wake up to an important issue.

WHAT IS A LETTER TO THE EDITOR?

A letter to the editor is a letter sent to a publication about issues of concern from its readers. Usually, letters are intended for publication. A letter to the editor is typically shorter than an op-ed.

It's written in direct response to an article previously published in that paper rather than any general news topic.

Letters to the editor have a longer history behind them. They've existed nearly as long as print newspapers. Just like op-eds, they are open to the public to be written, and there is no age restriction.

HOW TO WRITE AN OP-ED OR A LETTER TO THE EDITOR.

To write an op-ed or a letter to the editor, you need to have a strong and interesting opinion to share about something pertinent to the news or a major current issue. Your op-ed or letter, if written persuasively, can perhaps reach thousands if not millions of people. A well-written op-ed or letter has the power to shape minds, win over hearts, and maybe even have a concrete impact on politics and public policy.

Duke University put out a wonderful step-by-step guide to writing an op-ed. Even though this Duke guide is aimed at their students and alumni, you don't have to be a graduate from a prestigious university to write a kick-ass op-ed. Here is what you need to know:

1. **Track the news and jump at opportunities:** *"Timing is essential. When an issue is dominating the news, that's what readers want to read and op-ed editors want to publish. Whenever possible, link your issue explicitly to something happening in the news."* For example, a recent local natural disaster that is linked to climate change is a pertinent current event, and you can use it to illustrate why tackling the climate crisis is so important in your op-ed. If there has just been a hate-crime incident in the news, you can write an op-ed about the importance of

tackling discrimination and how those issues affect you in your daily life.

2. **Limit the article to 750 words:** *"Shorter is even better. Newspapers have limited space to offer, and editors generally won't take the time to cut a long article down to size."* You have to make your point concise. Submitting an article that is more than 750 words is setting yourself up for rejection. I know you have a lot to say (I am a very wordy person and cutting down my op-eds is always super painful), but you gotta make it short!

3. **Make a single point—well:** *"You cannot solve all of the world's problems in 750 words. Be satisfied with making a single point clearly and persuasively. If you cannot explain your message in a sentence or two, you're trying to cover too much."* I know you have so much to say, especially as a young person who typically is not given an outlet to express everything you've gone through and care about. But an op-ed is not your chance to talk about everything. It's just a single idea to focus on—you will have more opportunities for everything else you've been dying to express in other op-eds and writings.

4. **Put your main point at the top:** *"You have no more than 10 seconds to hook a busy reader, which means you shouldn't 'clear your throat' with a witticism or historical aside. Just get to the point and convince the reader that it's worth their valuable time to continue [reading]."* Make your point immediately, and hook them in fast! This isn't like an essay at school, where your teacher is going to read it anyway, whether or not you have a good introduction. Editors have no obligation to read each article submitted to them. If they are bored within the first few sentences, they will likely not even bother to read the rest of it.

5. **Tell readers why they should care:** *"Put yourself in the place of the busy person looking at your article. At the end of every few*

paragraphs, ask out loud: 'So what? Who cares?' You need to answer these questions. Appeals to self-interest usually are more effective than abstract punditry." Even though it's obvious to you why your issue matters, your readers probably don't have the same opinions and lived experiences. You need to put them in your shoes and really give them a reason to care, which often means spelling things out for them. Let them know exactly why it matters to you and why it should matter to them. Specific, relatable content is a lot better than abstract explanations that assume your readers already care about what you do.

6. **Offer specific recommendations:** *"An op-ed is not a news story that simply describes a situation; it is your opinion about how to improve matters. In an op-ed article you need to offer recommendations. How exactly should your state protect its environment, or the White House change its foreign policy, or parents choose healthier foods for their children? You'll need to do more than call for 'more research!' or suggest that opposing parties work out their differences."* This is not a research paper where you only list the facts as they have happened. This is your chance to speculate, to voice your ideas about the solution to the problem you are addressing.

7. **Embrace your personal voice:** *"The best of these examples will come from your own experience."* No academic degree is worth your own lived experiences. Someone can study what it's like to live as, for example, a young gay woman in America, but their research is nothing compared to our actual experiences as LGBTQ+ women. What you have gone through, what you know because it happened in your own life, your own story, is your power. Don't ever let anyone tell you that you are not an expert in your own lived experiences, and don't ever let anyone shut you down. You know your story, you know your power, and those who try to shut you down and claim they know more than you about your own experiences are lying.

As a gay girl, I know what it's like to encounter everyday homophobia mixed with misogyny more than any straight person in a library reading book after book about the gay struggle in America, researching their senior thesis. Whatever your lived experiences are, they are yours, and you are an expert in them. Don't neglect to show your readers your humanity and tell them honest stories of your own life pertinent to the point you're making.

But also acknowledge your own boundaries and know that you do not *have* to share everything. Exposing your pain and trauma so that others can learn is difficult emotional work that you don't have to take on, and you're not obligated to do it. Your own well-being and comfort are most important, so if telling your full experience feels like you are exploiting yourself and your own story, don't share it. Storytelling should feel rewarding and empowering. Draw a line in the sand for yourself, and set boundaries. I know a lot of queer people, people of color, and people of other marginalized identities often feel like we have to sacrifice our own well-being to be a living example and educator for those who don't share our experiences. Remember, you don't owe anyone anything. Yes, your story is important and has value being shared, but it is also *yours*.

8. **Play up your personal connection to the readers:** *"Daily newspapers in many cities are struggling to survive. As they compete with national publications, television, blogs, and others, they are playing up their local roots and coverage. Op-ed editors at these papers increasingly prefer authors who live locally or have other local connections. If you're submitting an article to your local paper, this will work in your favor. If you're submitting it in a city where you once lived or worked, be sure to mention this in your cover note and byline. Likewise, if you're writing for a publication that serves a particular profession, ethnic group or other cohort, let them know*

how you connect personally to their audience." You have to know who your audience is, who you're writing to, and appeal to them in the most authentic way possible.

9. **Use short sentences and paragraphs:** *"Look at some op-ed articles and count the number of words per sentence. You'll probably find the sentences to be quite short. You should use the same style, relying mainly on simple declarative sentences. Cut long paragraphs into two or more shorter ones."* Imagine you're scrolling through your newsfeed: Are you more likely to read a long, wordy article with big paragraphs that go on forever or one that looks short and approachable? Write what you would read. What kind of article would catch your attention and make you stop scrolling and pay attention?

10. **Avoid jargon:** *"If a technical detail is not essential to your argument, don't use it. When in doubt, leave it out. Simple language doesn't mean simple thinking; it means you are being considerate of readers who lack your expertise and are sitting half-awake at their breakfast table or computer screen."* Remember—writing an op-ed is *not* like writing an essay for your English class! You are not trying to impress a teacher by fitting in as many fancy words as you can find. You are getting a concise political point out into the world that you want anyone and everyone to be able to understand without having to google. Make your writing accessible for everyone.

11. **Use the active voice:** *"Don't write: 'It is hoped that [or: One would hope that] the government will…' Instead, say 'I hope the government will…' Active voice is nearly always better than passive voice. It's easier to read, and it leaves no doubt about who is doing the hoping, recommending or other action."* An active voice in writing shows urgency and power, expresses direct actions, and takes responsibility for your own statements. A passive voice is one that shies away from taking responsibility for your own

statements. Don't dance around the main point you're trying to make. This is your chance to bravely say everything you've been yelling at the TV when watching the news. You don't have to be timid—no matter how old you are, no matter what status you occupy in society, you can go ahead and point a finger at power and say, "You need to do XYZ differently!" That's what this whole *Youth to Power* thing is about anyway—using your voice to speak truth to power. Don't dance around what you want to say. If you want to directly call someone in power out or decry something that is happening, call them out by name!

12. **Avoid tedious rebuttals:** *"If you've written your article in response to an earlier piece that made your blood boil, avoid the temptation to prepare a point-by-point rebuttal. It makes you look petty. It's likely that readers didn't see the earlier article and, if they did, they've probably forgotten it. So, just take a deep breath, mention the earlier article once and argue your own case. If you really need to rebut the article, forego an op-ed article and instead write a letter to the editor, which is more appropriate for this purpose."* This applies more to crafting a letter to the editor, which is written in response to a previous article. You have a limited amount of words to get your point across, so save your words for making a statement, not being petty or tearing the other article down point by point. Save that for Twitter.

13. **Acknowledge the other side:** *"People writing op-ed articles sometimes make the mistake of piling on one reason after another why they're right and their opponents are wrong, if not idiots. They'd probably appear more credible, and almost certainly more humble and appealing, if they took a moment to acknowledge the ways in which their opponents are right. When you see experienced op-ed authors saying 'to be sure,' that's what they're doing."* This doesn't mean justify the other side. For topics like climate denial and white supremacy, the "other side" is nothing but

harmful propaganda. So if there are any credible, logical, or easy-to-understand points on the other side, acknowledge them and their reasoning. If the "other side" is nothing but ugly prejudice and lies and there is no nuance you can acknowledge as right on their end, you can skip this step.

14. **Make your ending a winner:** *"As noted, you need a strong opening paragraph, or 'lead,' to hook readers. When writing for the op-ed page, it's also important to summarize your argument in a strong final paragraph. That's because many casual readers scan the headline, skim the opening and then read the final paragraph and byline. In fact, one trick many columnists use is to conclude with a phrase or thought that appeared in the opening, thereby closing the circle."* Kind of like when writing an essay for school, the ending should restate the thesis. However, you need to get out of the school mind-set when writing your op-ed. This is supposed to be a lot more concise, entertaining, and powerful than any old-school essay, so make sure you end with a statement that really hits hard. Something powerful that sums up the point you're making and leaves people thinking. It doesn't hurt to make it quotable—something people copy and paste into their content when they retweet your amazing article!

15. **Relax and have fun:** *"Many authors, particularly academics, approach an op-ed article as an exercise in solemnity. Frankly, they'd improve their chances if they'd lighten up, have some fun and entertain the reader a bit."* This is not the time to be boring and scholarly. This is the time to be yourself on paper. Newspaper editors are always looking for that distinct youth voice. This is not the time to act like someone older than you are or go out of your way to be more solemn, controlled, and mature than someone your age. The whole point and power of your letter is getting the important but neglected youth voice out in the world.

ADDITIONAL TIPS SPECIFICALLY FOR WRITING A LETTER TO THE EDITOR

- **Cite the article you're responding to:** Don't expect the reader or editor to just know; no one reads every article ever. In fact no one, not even a newspaper editor, reads every single article in their own publication.

- **Keep it shorter and sweeter:** You need to be even more focused on your topic when writing a letter to the editor, because you have even less space to make your point. Because your letter is a response to another article, this should shape the focus of your work.

- **Make it timely, and be quick!** The newspaper you're writing to isn't interested in your response to a story published a month ago. You have to write and submit it the same day or the day after the article you are responding to is published. Newspapers are all about breaking the news—they're not interested in reporting on old stuff.

Okay...phew, you did it! You wrote a jaw-dropping, powerful op-ed, making an important case to the world. You are ready to infiltrate the adult-dominated media. But then you realize...*Oh wait, I actually need to submit this to a publication! How on earth do I do that?!*

HOW TO PITCH YOURSELF TO A PUBLICATION

1. **Compile a list of publications:** Go online and search every newspaper and magazine that could be best for your op-ed. Don't just aim for the big-name newspapers like the *New York Times* or the *Washington Post,* which have thousands of people pitching them all the time. Make a list that includes local newspapers and specialized publications that are more likely to appreciate your work and publish it, and reach out to

them. Having more articles published in local and small-scale publications not only ups your chances of having a larger publication pick up your work and reprint it, but it makes an impact in your community. The goal is not publishing in the most prestigious magazine; it's getting your message across to those who need to hear it. People in your community who read the local paper and magazines or other forms of news online are a great place to start. Make sure you know what the publication you are submitting your writing to typically covers, and aim for publications that make sense paired with your article. A sports magazine is less likely to feature an op-ed about war crimes in Yemen than a journal of military history.

2. **Read and research their publication guidelines carefully:** For every publication you are going to submit to, read through their guidelines and instructions for submission. They each have different things they would like you to include in the email you send them and formats they want you to use for documents. Also make sure that your writing fits within the word limit. I know *Youth to Power* is all about breaking rules that need to be broken, but when it comes to submitting your writing to a newspaper, website, or magazine, you want to increase your chances of publication by following their guidelines.

3. **Draft a sample email and find the right contact info:** For each publication you are submitting to, write an email according to their guidelines, and *never* just cc all the emails of the publications you want to submit your writing to. Don't send your pitch in one massive email chain. Each publication needs to receive a short and sweet individualized email from you telling them who you are, any credentials you have, and

why they should publish your writing. Here is an example of a successful pitch I made to the *Seattle Times*, one of the first op-eds that I ever had published. I was about fourteen years old.

This is the actual email I sent to the *Seattle Times* editor:

Dear Editor,

As a fourteen-year-old-girl, watching the events of the second presidential debate have been more than disturbing for me. The news cycles seem to have already moved on from the debate, but I'm still reeling. What we all saw on TV on Sunday was not okay, and has more value than we're giving it.

I've previously published two articles in "The Writer's Dig," which is a blog on Writer's Digest viewed by roughly a million people: *Teen Writers Come of Age* and *What NOT to Do When Writing YA Books (Advice from a Teen Writer)*. My articles, *Sitting Out*, and *Not Just Ribbons and Rhinestones*, were published in Teen Ink's monthly print magazine.

Sincerely,
Jamie Margolin

In this letter, I explained how as a young person I had a unique and important perspective on a pressing current event, and I listed some of my past published writing. If you haven't published anything before, that is totally okay! Everyone has to start somewhere! You can also mention details like working on your school newspaper or other relevant extracurriculars. But it's also not mandatory or necessary to mention any credentials. The important thing to get across in this short email is your voice and why it needs to be heard on a timely topic.

4. **Do one last proofread:** Spell-check your email, and make sure your op-ed or letter to the editor is actually pasted in the email. Give your writing one last read, and make sure everything fits within the guidelines of the publications you are sending your writing to.

5. **Send!** Your voice deserves to be heard, your story is important, so close your eyes if you have to, and just click Send.

REJECTION

You're going to get rejected a bunch—welcome to the club! Fun fact: I have an entire Google Drive folder of rejection emails from all sorts of publications. (It's a *very* big folder.) Being rejected does NOT mean that your voice isn't important, that you should have never put yourself out there, that you aren't good enough, or any of those other thoughts that race through your mind when you get that dreaded "thanks but no thanks" email. I don't know a single writer or activist who hasn't been rejected at least five times. More like fifteen times. At *least*. Remember that newspapers and magazines are all about breaking news stories and getting readers, so if your writing does not fit with their publication, it's not personal.

Take those Ls and keep going! Keep submitting! Keep trying!

And if after a few weeks of emailing and trying, no one publishes your work—be your own publisher. Start a blog, post it there, and amplify your writing on social media. No matter what, your voice as a young person speaking truth to power and calling for change deserves to be out in the world.

Then write the next op-ed and try again. Publications will appreciate your tenacity and perseverance. Plus, the more you write, the more you hone your craft, refine your voice, and grow your confidence.

ACCEPTANCE

Your op-ed or letter to the editor got accepted for publication?

CONGRATULATIONS! Do a happy dance if that's your thing, and take a moment to let it sink in. Your voice, your story, and your unique lived experience as a young person are going to be heard in a very public way! It is worth keeping in mind that your work might be edited to make your points a little clearer or your writing more concise, so what is published may come out a bit different from what you wrote.

Also, make sure to research whether the publication that has accepted you pays their writers! I have had a few instances where a publisher usually paid their writers but wasn't going to compensate me because I never asked and they thought they could get by not paying me because I was young! Luckily, I asked them about compensation, and because I brought up money, they ended up paying me. You deserve to be paid for your work, so do your research!

Now, if you are someone who learns from looking at examples, here are some sample op-eds that I have published in various publications, for you to get a feel for how to craft an op-ed as a young person and a sense of the different kinds of topics.

This first op-ed was for my local newspaper, the *Seattle Times*, the result of that example email on page 35. Other than my Teen Ink blog posts, it was my first officially published article. It is short and sweet, but it gets a point across:

Published: October 2016

Presidential politics as seen by a 14-year-old

As a girl who aspires to be a politician in the future, Donald Trump's behavior has been very disturbing.

"OUR kids are watching this election" Michelle Obama said in a speech about the intensifying craziness of the 2016 presidential race. She's right. There are young people watching this election—I'm one of them.

The three debates between Donald Trump and Hillary Clinton have been considered the most nasty presidential debates in recent history. And I couldn't agree more. With each one, it took willpower not to chuck my remote at the TV.

One of the main things that made the debates so insufferable was the way Trump threw basic etiquette out the window. He constantly interrupted Clinton and made all sorts of power moves, such as stalking her around the town hall stage, invading her personal space.

In contrast, Clinton was poised and polite. For the most part, she sat quietly and waited calmly for her opponent to finish talking, smiling at the attacks thrown at her. Clinton's class in the face of such a bully made me respect her that much more—but it also made me furious.

It's so insulting that someone like Trump is even on the same stage as Clinton. The fact that a woman who has spent her entire adult life in public service has to be put on an even playing field with a man who tweets about alleged sex tapes at 3 a.m. is proof that the double standard is still alive.

As a girl who aspires to be a politician in the future, I find that very disturbing.

But the most disgusting part of the debates was how much Trump got away with. He dismissed his sexual-assault boasting by claiming, "Bill Clinton is worse" (implying that a woman is more responsible for her husband's actions from 20 years ago than a man is for his own actions from 11 years ago).

He has admitted that he does not pay federal income tax. Yet through it all, the media are cutting him slack. After each meltdown, reporters talked about how he could "prove himself" with his next debate performance.

Prove what, I'd like to ask? What is everyone waiting for him to do? I mean, if a candidate targeting minorities, encouraging violence, bragging about sexual assault and refusing to accept the fair outcome of an election isn't enough for us, then, my gosh, nothing ever will be.

We shouldn't be giving people like Trump "opportunities" to "change our minds." What's done is done. Debate results are subjective, and performances don't change the facts. And they shouldn't change our minds.

The next op-ed was for the *Guardian*. Unlike the *Seattle Times* op-ed, this one wasn't just about making a political statement. I told a story of something that I was going through as a young person living in the Pacific Northwest, feeling the effects of climate change. Op-eds don't have to just state an opinion. You can talk about something you've done or an action you've taken. Op-eds can be a form of half news/half storytelling, and stories are always compelling to both readers and publishers. Take a look:

Published: October 2018

I sued the state of Washington because I can't breathe there. They ignored me.

Summers in my home city of Seattle didn't used to be smoggy to the point that they make me and my friends sick. Now they are— and that violates our rights

I was born after 9/11, so extensive airport security has always been a reality for me. So has the fact that life as we know it on this planet is coming to an end because of climate change, and that my generation will inherit a looming apocalyptic-scale disaster.

My name is Jamie, I'm 16 years old, I'm going into my junior year of high school, and I, along with 12 other young people, recently sued the state of Washington. Why? Because Governor Jay Inslee and the whole state government is screwing over my generation.

Washington state's elected officials talk about solving the climate crisis, but then turn around and issue permits for fossil fuel plants that poison communities, and destroy the ecosystems, water, air and land that my generation

39

and future generations need to survive.

The even crazier part is that they are destroying our life support systems with a fossil fuel energy system that is wholly unnecessary to provide for our basic energy needs. Experts across the planet say that we don't need to power our planet with dirty life-threatening fuels.

Summers in my home city of Seattle didn't use to be smoggy to the point that they make me and my friends sick. In fact, they didn't use to be smoggy and smoke-filled at all. But now, when I scroll through my Instagram feed in the summer, instead of seeing pictures of my friends enjoying the sun, I see some of them wearing gas masks above captions saying things like "I can't find breathable air anywhere." I also see pictures of what is supposed to be the Seattle skyline, but all you can see is smoke.

Smoke from the fires in Canada—worsened by unusually hot and dry summers—have made the air quality on the worst days worse than in Beijing. The winds blow the smoke down over the Pacific North-West, suffocating us.

There was a week in August where I didn't dare to step outside. It was grey 24/7—not from clouds, but from smoke. If I went outside,

it hurt to breathe, the air smelled funny, and I got a headache and sore throat. This is not the way it used to be in my home town.

I'm able-bodied, so for my friends with chronic health conditions, it's even worse. A few had to go to the ER for respiratory emergencies caused by the smoke. My city is suffocating every summer. The whole Pacific North-West can't breathe.

In the US Constitution it says that everyone has the rights to life, liberty and the pursuit of happiness. Washington state law says that I have a "fundamental and inalienable right to a healthful environment." But how am I supposed to live my life and pursue happiness when I can't go outside in the summer and am living on a planet where record-breaking storms, epidemic wildfires, and heat waves are displacing, sickening, and killing thousands?

That's why, with the help of the non-profit organization Our Children's Trust, 12 other youth and I sued the state of Washington for denying young people our constitutional rights to life, liberty and the pursuit of happiness by actively worsening the climate crisis.

Last week we got a ruling from the court that was pretty

much a complete write-off to my generation and kids everywhere who apparently now have to be "optimistic" and beg our leaders for rights so basic as a livable planet. Rights that previous generations were able to enjoy.

The ruling granted the state's motion to dismiss our case. Instead of supporting young people asking for a livable future, the state fought tooth and nail to shut us down, and the court ruled in favor of silencing the young people's pleas.

What's even more disappointing is that the judge ignored the fact that the legislature has already stated that the youth have a "fundamental and inalienable" right to a "healthful environment." Here is what the law says: "The legislature recognizes that each person has a fundamental and inalienable right to a healthful environment and that each person has a responsibility to contribute to the preservation and enhancement of the environment." This is the only right the legislature has characterized as "fundamental and inalienable."

The judge who ruled on this case did not assume that the scientific facts we put in the complaint were true, which is what he was supposed to do. He instead relied upon his personal opinions and outside sources for the proposition that the youth should be "optimistic" about their futures and hope that the ruling generation will change course. *Optimistic.* How in the world am I supposed to be optimistic when I am literally being given warnings not to go outside and breathe the air because it is unhealthy? Apparently he neglected to look outside his window to see how wildfire smoke has plagued our city.

When youth try to take a stand, our leaders blatantly and explicitly disregard our rights, pat us on the head, and give us the legal equivalent of "you're cute, don't worry about a thing little kid, we're taking care of it." But the Washington state government isn't taking care of anything when it comes to climate action.

My generation's right to a healthful environment is not an "aspiration," as the judge said. My own legislature has already recognized this as a right that must be protected: "The legislature recognizes that each person has a fundamental and inalienable right to a healthful environment and that each person has a responsibility to contribute to the preservation and enhancement of the environment." This is the only right the legislature has characterized as "fundamental and inalienable."

The constitution requires the judicial branch to serve as a check and balance of executive and legislative actions that are unconstitutional. This principle was used to challenge laws that segregated African American children in public education, laws that prevented same-sex couples from marrying and laws that prevent meaningful suffrage.

Youth being harmed by climate change are entitled to the same kind of consideration. We won't stop fighting until we get the change we need and deserve.

I hope those examples help. But I am just one person, with one set of life experiences and opinions. For more examples from a more diverse set of writing styles, you can just google "op-eds by youth" or just the names of your favorite youth activists and read as many as you need to get a feel for it!

No matter where you are and what resources you have access to (if you don't own a computer, go to a library and write your masterpiece there)—you can use your writing to change the world.

Devin Halbal, Twenty, She/Her
Transgender rights and community support activist,
intern at the LGBT Center of NYC, freelance writer

JAMIE: **How did you become an activist?**

DEVIN: Growing up I identified as he/him because I was
assigned male at birth. In high school I was experiencing
really bad mental health problems because I didn't
know I was trans. Once I graduated, I began to realize
I was a transgender girl, and I began to transition.
Because of this, I was attacked on the train.

After that, I was looking for a way to share my story
and to educate people on the harsh realities of being a
trans woman of color in a big city. I wrote an editorial in
Teen Vogue.

Then I took my activism into my community, working
at my local LGBT center. I lead trans support groups,
because trans people don't know about the resources
that New York City has for them in terms of health care
and mental health services.

JAMIE: **What is your advice for other young activists?**

DEVIN: Focus on what you want to change and what your
talent is. If you're into medicine, you can take action
there.

There are many ways to create community in your city
and state. Find people similar to you and create support
systems and organize events.

Do not depend on publications to make the art you want. If your writing and artwork is not accepted, use the internet and social media and self-publish.

JAMIE: **What do you say to LGBTQ+ kids who want to be activists but are not safe to come out?**

DEVIN: If you are existing in this world as queer, thank you for existing visibly and publicly and loudly. Being queer and trans and being visible can be dangerous, so figure out your timing. Allow yourself to share that bit of your identity with certain people and spaces.

Writing down your feelings and reflecting on who you are is important. I think about the people that came before me. I think about how beautiful it is to be queer and how beautiful my perspective is in a world where people don't have that.

Go to a clinic, nonprofits, and support groups. Surround yourself with community because it can make living in this world way less lonely.

Use social media to talk about your experiences under a pseudonym. You can be anonymous online and not associate your activism with your name. By sharing your art and writing online anonymously, you can participate in the LGBT+ community and liberation movement without endangering and outing yourself.

4

HEADING UP YOUR OWN MOVEMENT

TAKING YOUR ACTIVISM TO THE NEXT LEVEL AND BUILDING SOMETHING YOURSELF.

I like to think of activism and different changemaking spaces like an ecosystem. Not every living organism can perform every job needed in their ecosystem. In a forest ecosystem, one organism does not photosynthesize, eat plants to keep their populations in check, hunt, fertilize, produce oxygen, *and* decompose waste at the same time; in the changemaking world, one organization or movement does not fulfill everyone's needs and accomplish every goal. In a forest, the deer, squirrels, grass, trees, and birds coexist and serve different purposes in their ecosystem. Together, they form a healthy habitat collaborating and feeding off each other. Although they all serve separate purposes in the forest, they do not go their separate ways. Each animal and plant species helps the others survive, and there is an intricate web of connections and relationships that go far beyond what meets the eye.

In changemaking, the women's rights movement, environmental and climate justice movement, indigenous rights movement,

Black Lives Matter movement, reproductive rights movement and feminist movement, LGBTQ+ movement, health-care and disability rights movement, and labor justice movement live in an ecosystem together. Within each movement is an ecosystem of its own.

There are different niches to be filled within the environmental movement. For example, there are organizations that do legal writing, groups that organize protests and direct action, and campaigns to lobby politicians and change public opinion, and on and on. Each movement has an intricate web of advocacy groups, organizations, activists, law firms, public relations firms, grassroots organizers, journalists, artists, and more who make the movement robust.

Individual communities also have their own ecosystems of grassroots movements. A community might have a Planned Parenthood, local workers' union, environmental and cleanup advocacy group, and others that make up the fabric of the movement space in their area.

This chapter is all about starting something new: beginning a new organization, movement, or campaign that is missing from your ecosystem. To start something new that will be meaningful and contribute to the greater good of the community and cause you're fighting for, you have to get in touch with your *why* and see how that ties into the ecological niche you're filling. It is important to be aware of all the ecosystems that you are a part of: the larger changemaking ecosystem, the ecosystem of the movement you work in, and your community's ecosystem. Know the part you play, the ecological niche you fill, and be mindful of the work others are doing.

Now that we have a framework for what the changemaking landscape looks like, let's jump into how you know when it's time to fill a new niche.

Let's say you've been dabbling in other organizations and activities, researching your options, but you feel like something is missing. No one is taking the course of action you have in mind. Your community is in need of resources, support, or other services that are not currently being provided. The movement space you are working in is not giving you the freedom you need to take the kind of action you believe in, or you have felt unwelcome and unrepresented in other organizations. Whatever it is, something is missing, and you want to fill that gap. This is how you start your own movement/organization. I will use the example of the organization I started when I was fifteen, Zero Hour, and how we got started to show you a real example of a youth movement built from the ground up.

I can tell you right now that building your own movement is not easy. It takes a lot of hard work, sweat, and tears, but it is *so* worth it. Are you up for it? Let's do this!

MOVEMENT AND ORGANIZATION BUILDING 101

1. **Identify a need and a clear idea of filling that need:** What is missing? What strategy is the movement you are a part of not taking? What voices are being left out? What approach hasn't been tried yet that you believe should? What topic are people not educated on?

HOW ZERO HOUR CAME TO BE

The problem: A total lack of global urgency about the climate crisis and protecting the lives and futures of young people. Back in 2017, climate change and climate justice were being completely left out of the mainstream media, and there was a lack of urgency about the climate crisis in politics, the private sector, and the general public. The environmental movement also had a lot of problems with diversity and racism, and there was no official national space for young women and young people of color to lead in the broader American climate movement.

The solution: Zero Hour, an international youth climate march and lobby day to capture international attention about the urgency of the climate crisis, organized by a climate justice organization run and led mostly by young women.

2. **Find your people:** How you go about this depends on what kind of action you want to take. Sometimes, starting a movement can be an individual feat. In late September 2018, then-fifteen-year-old Greta Thunberg of Sweden sat in front of the Swedish parliament with a sign that said "School Strike for Climate" and launched an international climate strike youth movement phenomenon. Sometimes you don't need to go out of your way to find your people; you can fill that gap and start a revolution by yourself. But most of the time, you're going to need a team: people who believe in your vision and are willing to join you to make it happen.

You find your team by spreading your message, communicating what you want to accomplish, and asking people to join you. Recruit folks over social media, at events, with one-on-one conversations—it's all about finding people with the same vision as you who will take time out of their day to make something come to life. That was how I found a team to make the 2018 Youth Climate March, and later Zero Hour, come to life.

How I Found My Zero Hour Team

When the idea to start the Youth Climate March solidified in my head, I first was too scared to act on an idea so big. Where does one even start mobilizing thousands of youth for climate action when you have no huge influence or number of followers? When you're just some kid? So I pushed the idea down, right up until the summer of 2017, when climate disasters like Hurricane Maria in Puerto Rico struck and the media and politicians refused to address them. Around that time, my city of Seattle was coated in a thick blanket of smog due to climate-worsened wildfires. A few bad-air-quality migraines and climate-disaster panic attacks later, and I decided, *Screw it, I'm going to make this happen.*

In the summer of 2017 I took to Instagram to make the announcement. I posted a picture of a sign that said, "The Youth March on Washington," a reference to Dr. Martin Luther King Jr.'s March on Washington, and I wrote that I was going to organize a youth climate march. I asked whoever wanted to make the vision come to life to direct message me.

I received a single direct message from an internet friend of mine, Nadia Nazar. She was fifteen at the time, and we'd been talking on Instagram ever since she read an op-ed of mine that was published in a student magazine. Nadia said, "I'm in," and she was the first person to hop on board and be my partner in making this march a reality. It's funny how it was almost fate. If I had not written that op-ed for a student magazine, if Nadia's teacher had not known she was interested in environmental action and made her read the piece, if Nadia had not taken the time to follow her teacher's recommendation and read that article, if Nadia had not been inclined to look me up on Instagram after she read it and send me a message, Zero Hour and the Youth Climate March might have never come to life. I am a believer in things falling into place, but you have to *make* them fall into place. If you put out hard work and energy and a killer vision and idea, people will want to join you.

Nadia lived in Baltimore, and I lived in Seattle. Even though we were on opposite sides of the country, I think I spoke more to Nadia over that year of organizing than I did to my own parents. I started having phone calls with her to plan out the march several times a day, and I brought in two people I met at a summer program, Madelaine Tew and Zanagee Artis.

The rest of the team came together because Nadia and I communicated a strong vision for the movement and the march everywhere we went. We talked about it at events, in one-on-one conversations with friends, and on social media, and I sent out tons of emails to adult activists I admired to help mentor us.

The first adult to respond was Mrinalini Chakraborty from the Women's March, and she agreed to mentor this broke group of young people with nothing but a big dream and killer work ethic. After Mrinalini helped us get a website up, another adult joined and helped us get a fiscal sponsor so we could start raising money. Then more youth heard about us and joined. Then I went to a conference and won over Natalie Mebane, a DC environmental lobbyist who after one conversation with me agreed to join the movement. Soon we had a constant influx of interest and a team full of badass young women (mostly of color) and women of color mentors working toward a climate justice revolution.

To build a good team, you have to be clear about your vision and what it is you are building; you can't just expect people to fall into your lap. You have to go out of your way to convince and recruit—one conversation can change everything. It sure changed everything for Zero Hour. We got two of our most helpful, wise, and dedicated adult mentors by two great conversations. After just a phone call, Shravya Jain, a climate media expert from Climate Nexus, joined the Zero Hour team and saved us with her expertise in press strategy. Be genuine, and you will attract the right people. Sell the movement, sell yourself, and if the idea and vision are solid, people will join.

3. **Write a mission and vision statement:** Okay. So you have your idea, and you have your people to help make it happen. It's time to get down exactly what you want to accomplish and what your vision is for your movement going forward. Writing down a unifying vision and mission statement that the whole team agrees on and comes back to periodically is an important way of staying grounded in your original purpose and of communicating your mission to the world. To clarify, a mission statement is what your organization/movement is essentially on a mission to create and what you want to be, and your vision statement is about your vision for the world you're trying to build. Here are Zero Hour's mission and vision statements that we as a team wrote out before the Youth Climate March in 2018. We do not edit and reevalutate our mission and vision statements often, only if there is a major shift in the direction of the organization and it needs some revisiting.

THE ZERO HOUR MISSION STATEMENT

The mission of Zero Hour is to center the voices of diverse youth in the conversation around climate and environmental justice. Zero Hour is a youth-led movement creating entry points, training, and resources for new young activists and organizers (and adults who support our vision) wanting to take concrete action around climate change. Together, we are a movement of unstoppable youth organizing to protect our rights and access to the natural resources and a clean, safe, and healthy environment that will ensure a livable future where we not just survive, but flourish.

THE ZERO HOUR VISION STATEMENT

Enough is enough. We, the youth, believe that #ThisIsZero-Hour to act on climate change. We cannot afford to wait any longer for adults to protect our right to the clean and safe environment, the natural resources we need to not just survive, but flourish. We know that we are the leaders we have been waiting for! We believe that every individual, from every community should have access to clean air, water, and public lands. We believe in putting the needs and health of our communities before corporate gain. We believe that the leadership of youth in this space is essential because we have inherited a crisis that we had no hand in creating. We will strive to hold our adults and elected officials accountable for their legacy of destruction and inaction when it comes climate change. We believe in a solutions-based approach that addresses the real needs of our communities. While climate change is a phenomenon that will impact all of us—if it has not already—we believe that the impact of the climate crisis is profoundly unequal. Frontline communities across the globe and within the United States have been directly impacted by climate change to a degree greater than others. We believe, however, that those closest to the problem are also often closest to the solution. These communities have been actively working to create just solutions and transitions. Our goal is to center the unique wisdom, experience, and leadership of these communities in our efforts to make impactful change. We also recognize that a movement for climate and environmental justice cannot be successful without building meaningful coalitions and cross-sector alignment with other movements for social justice. We believe in harnessing the power of youth-led organizing and leadership by youth from different backgrounds and experiences in forging our path toward a more equitable and safe future for all of us.

4. **Establish an internal structure, rules, and democracy:** It is important for there to be a rhyme and reason to the way your movement functions. Democracy and structure are essential to the success of every movement, because if you are fighting

for justice, there has to be fairness in the way you operate. Take the time with your team to outline an internal structure, rules of how you operate, and what your democracy looks like. It won't be the most glamorous part of organizing, but trust me, you're going to be glad you did.

I'm going to be completely honest with you when I say this was *not* easy for Zero Hour, and honestly, we're still working on it every day. This step in movement building requires a lot of active listening, exhausting conference calls, meetings that can last for hours, and sometimes arguing and hard feelings. Tension is normal, and I've sure had a lot of it in my movement-building experiences. People tend to get *very* passionate about their experiences, and unlike having ideas for a normal job, with movement building, it tends to get a whole lot more personal. Oftentimes, organizers see our work not as separate from us but as an extension of our being, so when our ideas get turned down or someone else pushes an idea or structure that we disagree with, it's easy for the situation to get emotional.

This stage in movement building requires a lot of consideration and caution around other people's ideas, opinions, and feelings, as well as a lot of patience, compromise, and emotional labor. This is my very least favorite part of activism, because it's exhausting, and it can often feel so messy, like everything you're working on is falling apart. Even if your intention is not to offend, chances are someone somewhere is going to be unhappy with you. It's impossible to make everyone happy, and let me just warn you, this process isn't pretty.

There are many different ways you can go about structuring decision making on these topics and in general for your organization/movement. The most common method in grassroots organizations is consensus-based decision making. What that means is that your decisions are based on general agreement. Consensus decision making is a creative and dynamic way of reaching agreement among all members of a group. Instead of simple majority rule, a group using consensus is committed to finding solutions that everyone actively supports or at least can live with. Consensus is 100 percent support, not 100 percent agreement. The reason why this is so important is that if you have people on your team who are strongly against the decision made, especially if they feel they haven't been heard, they will drag their feet, hold you back, and cause problems. For a handy visualization of the decision-making process, see the diagram on page 55.

BUILDING YOUR MOVEMENT

1. **Find your allies:** Remember that you are a part of a movement ecosystem. You are not organizing in a vacuum. This means that it is strategic to ask for help from partner organizations. Talk to other organizers about what you are starting and how you would like to collaborate with them. Remember, you are not competing with these other organizations; you are instead building on their work and collectively strengthening the cause. Just like in the natural world of mutually beneficial relationships in which multiple creatures, like bees and flowers, support and enrich each other's existence, you and other organizations can have mutually beneficial relationships that grow your movement and advance the cause. The more interconnected and in tune with each other members of a movement ecosystem are, the better chance you and your allies have of succeeding.

Decision Making Diagram

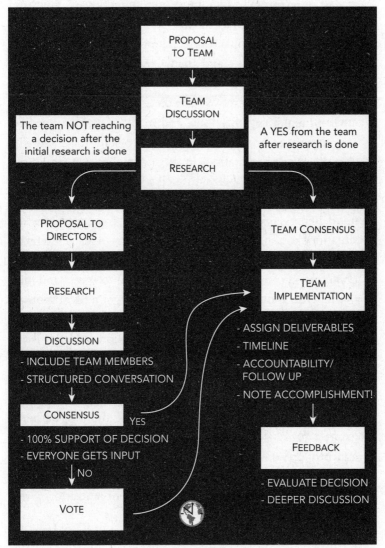

Credit: Nadia Nazar

ZERO HOUR'S ALLIES

To make the Youth Climate March in 2018 a success, we at Zero Hour mobilized not just our own followers but those of other organizations like the Sunrise Movement, the International Indigenous Youth Council, Rezpect Our Water (Standing Rock Kids), and many grassroots climate justice communities and organizations. We communicated our vision and what we were working on to other social justice and environmental organizations, and many of them signed on and endorsed our work. Without the collaboration and allyship of other organizations in the movement, we would not have been able to mobilize on such a large scale.

2. **Set up a way to receive donations and the resources you will need:** (This is my understanding based on my experience and situation. You should of course find your own legal and financial advisors.) If you are starting an organization or setting up any kind of initiative that requires you to spend and raise money, you should either incorporate or get a fiscal sponsor. What does this mean? Well, sorry to get technical, but this is all about taxes. In the United States, Section 501(c)(3) is the portion of the US Internal Revenue Code that allows for federal tax exemption of nonprofit organizations, specifically those that are considered public charities, private foundations, or private operating foundations. One of the biggest benefits of a 501(c)(3) is exemption from federal taxes, sales taxes, and property taxes. You may even be exempt from payroll taxes if you have employees. Being tax exempt will save you money over time, a plus to any nonprofit organization barely scraping by.

There are two ways you can achieve a 501(c)(3) status— by applying to "incorporate" yourself or by getting a fiscal sponsor—that is, working under the umbrella of another already existing 501(c)(3) that handles your finances for you but in return takes a small percentage of the money you make.

A third route is to become or be fiscally sponsored by a 501(c)(4), which is similar to a 501(c)(3) except it allows you to engage more with the political system and endorse candidates, whereas a 501(c)(3) does not.

Zero Hour's Finances

At the moment, Zero Hour operates financially through a fiscal sponsor that handles our finances, taxes, and all of that nitty-gritty legal money stuff so the other high schoolers and I don't have to. People get super squeamish when it comes to money and youth, and that's why at first it was a little tricky finding a fiscal sponsor to take us on as its fiscal responsibility. Now their director of operations helps us stay on top of our finances, advises us on wise financial decisions, and stops people from taking advantage of us.

As a young person or a youth-run organization, you are prone to being taken advantage of financially all the time. Because youth don't have the same financial and business knowledge as full-grown adults with degrees and experience in the field, that makes us easy targets. Sometimes it doesn't come from a malicious place as much as it does from a *These cute kids are too young to have any large quantity of money* kind of way. Our fiscal sponsor has experience and expertise in finances and can spot whenever someone is trying to give us the short end of the stick just because we are kids.

3. **Make a timeline and execute it:** Between now and your first goal, make a timeline for each main section of your movement/organization. Make a fundraising timeline, a media and social media timeline, an outreach timeline, and so on. Be

realistic when making this outline, and then stick to it. Time-lines help you and your team organize yourselves and plan strategically to achieve success. Use this outline as a template timeline that can be tailored for any task.

ZERO HOUR'S YOUTH CLIMATE MARCH
FUNDRAISING TIMELINE

This is a directly copy-and-pasted, verbatim timeline that our finance team, run by the then-sixteen-year-old finance director, Madelaine Tew, put together for the 2018 Youth Climate March and Youth Climate Lobby Day.

Disclaimer: We did not end up hitting our target of raising $250,000 for the Youth Climate March. Sometimes this happens! We had not proven ourselves as an organization yet, so we had to scrape together what we could and pull off the best action possible with what was at our disposal. We were able to pull off our actions with $80,000, which we raised entirely through grants the finance team painstakingly applied for and through grassroots donations.

ZERO HOUR 2018 FUNDRAISING STRATEGY

I. The Goal
    A. Raise $250,000 for the lobby day and march.
        1. Actual needs are around $200,000, but we are aiming for $250,000 to be safe.
    B. Incorporate bare minimum (internally).
II. The Mission
    A. This money is for programmatic purposes; see budget for specifics on what we need for the march and other.
III. Sources
    A. Corporations:

1. This will be our first stream of funds; more likely to give us money at a starting point than foundations or individual donors.
2. While we do this, the partnership teams should be sending out requests to our established donors (be in communication with that team).
3. Materials: one-pager *(a one-page document defining your organization for funders)* and sponsorship deck *(a document outlining how your organization will appreciate and credit organizations, individual donor companies, and foundations that fund at different amounts).*

B. Foundations:
1. Once we reach $25,000 or 10% of the goal, we will be ready to start reaching out to foundations.
2. We don't have to have $25,000 in the bank, but at least confirmation that corporations have agreed to give us money.

C. Individuals:
1. This will be our last chronological stream.

IV. The Timeline
A. March:
1. Determine plan for fiscal sponsorship.
2. Discuss individual donorship.
3. Quarterly report.
4. Reach out to five donors.
5. Reach $5,000 on crowdfunding site.
6. Secure fundraising mentor (temporary position).

B. April: (corporations month)
1. Adjust budget to fit $250,000.
2. Discuss our approach to corporations with mentor.
3. Adjust budget to fit the lowest possible amount.

4. Add to and finish sponsorship deck.

5. Finish research on corporations.

6. Research foundations and work on sample Letter of Intent for grants.

7. Reach out to fifteen corporations.

8. Get confirmation from corporations.

9. Reach out to four big greens with sponsorship deck. *(A "big green" is climate movement slang for a large, well-funded, and well-established environmental nonprofit. Kind of like people say, "big oil," we in the climate movement say "big greens" when referring to the multimillion-dollar fully staffed powerful organizations within the movement.)*

10. Start reaching out to foundations—about five if time permits.

11. Reach a total of $15,000 on crowdfunding site.

12. Reach $50,000.

C. May: (foundations month)

1. Finalize and publish sponsored ads.

2. Work on and finalize customized LOIs and proposals for foundations (throughout May).

3. Continue to reach out to corporations if there are more hopeful prospects.

4. Reach out to twenty foundations through direct emails.

5. Adjust LOIs to fit the specific foundation.

6. Hopefully get on calls with foundations.

7. Follow up with foundations in email (1–2 days after call/email of interest).

8. If no response, follow up again to remind them in a professional way.

9. Hopefully submit a proposal.

10. Send out thank-you letters.

    11. Reach $100,000.

    12. Send foundations the first mini–progress report.

D. June: (individual month)

    1. Continue sending out introduction emails/LOIs/ proposals (throughout June).

    2. Finalize individuals pitch.

    3. Contact ten individuals.

    4. Send ten individuals follow-ups with the proper materials attached.

    5. Contact another ten individuals.

    6. Another ten follow-ups with the proper materials.

    7. Raise $75,000 to reach $175,000.

E. July: (spending month)

    1. Continue contacting individuals and corporations if more come up.

    2. Reach $200,000–$250,000.

    3. Rely on budget (low, medium, or high depending on amount raised) to start worrying about expenditures.

    4. March and lobby day!

4. **Recognize the shoulders you are standing on:** It can often feel very lonely starting something new, but you have to remember you are not organizing in a vacuum. You are a part of a large family of changemakers who have been fighting for justice long before you were born. They have had failures and victories you can learn from; they have whole strategies that took years of experience to cultivate. Build upon the knowledge of movements before you.

If you don't know where to start in terms of using strategies and principles that have been laid out by activists before you, try the *Jemez Principles of Democratic Organizing*. On December 6–8, 1996, forty people of color and European

American representatives met in Jemez, New Mexico, for the "Working Group Meeting on Globalization and Trade." The Jemez meeting was hosted by the Southwest Network for Environmental and Economic Justice with the intention of hammering out common understandings among participants from different cultures, politics, and organizations. The *Jemez Principles* were built for the environmental and economic justice movements, but they are an excellent guide for effectively and justly running pretty much all movements.

This is just one of many historical guides out there for organizing. Martin Luther King Jr.'s steps for nonviolent direct action is another I highly recommend. Read the literature, watch documentaries, and learn about past strategies so you can build upon them.

Jemez Principles of Democratic Organizing

#1 Be Inclusive

If we hope to achieve just societies that include all people in decision-making and assure that all people have an equitable share of the wealth and the work of this world, then we must work to build that kind of inclusiveness into our own movement in order to develop alternative policies and institutions to the treaties policies under neoliberalism. This requires more than tokenism; it cannot be achieved without diversity at the planning table, in staffing, and in coordination. It may delay achievement of other important goals, it will require discussion, hard work, patience, and advance planning. It may involve conflict, but through this conflict, we can learn better ways of working together. It's about building alternative institutions, movement building, and not compromising out in order to be accepted into the anti-globalization club.

#2 Emphasis on Bottom-Up Organizing

To succeed, it is important to reach out into new constituencies, and to reach within all levels of leadership and membership base of the organizations that are already involved in our networks. We must be continually building and strengthening a base which provides our credibility, our strategies, mobilizations, leadership development, and the energy for the work we must do daily.

#3 Let People Speak for Themselves

We must be sure that relevant voices of people directly affected are heard. Ways must be provided for spokespersons to represent and be responsible to the affected constituencies. It is important for organizations to clarify their roles, and who they represent, and to assure accountability within our structures.

#4 Work Together in Solidarity and Mutuality

Groups working on similar issues with compatible visions should consciously act in solidarity, mutuality, and support each other's work. In the long run, a more significant step is to incorporate the goals and values of other groups with your own work, in order to build strong relationships. For instance, in the long run, it is more important that labor unions and community economic development projects include the issue of environmental sustainability in their own strategies, rather than just lending support to the environmental organizations. So communications, strategies, and resource sharing are critical, to help us see our connections and build on these.

#5 Build Just Relationships Among Ourselves

We need to treat each other with justice and respect, both on an individual and an organizational level, in this country and across borders. Defining and developing "just relationships" will be a process that won't happen overnight. It must include clarity about decision-making, sharing strategies, and resource distribution. There are clearly many skills necessary to succeed, and we need to determine the ways for those with different skills to coordinate and be accountable to one another.

#6 Commitment to Self-Transformation

As we change societies, we must change from operating on the mode of individualism to community-centeredness. We must "walk our talk." We must be the values that we say we're struggling for and we must be justice, be peace, be community.

There are many other resources out there like the *Jemez Principles of Democratic Organizing* put together by coalitions of organizers that can help guide you in your organizing. Remember that you are standing on the shoulders of decades of movements that have been organizing and refining their techniques to bend the world toward positive change.

5. **Keep at it—and remember, it's okay to fail:** Lastly, you don't have to get it right the first try! Movement building is hard and complicated and often takes many attempts to get right. There will be so many times on your journey in building a movement that you will be tempted to throw in the towel and quit. There will be many moments where you feel like no one is listening. You simply have to block out those fears and keep chugging forward.

    Inspiration and enthusiasm will come and go. You have to manage the two extreme emotions of *I'm invincible* and *I can't do this* with a steady middle ground of strategically and analytically chugging ahead.

Learn from your mistakes, and by all means take a step back and change your strategy if something isn't working. Keep failing and failing until you get it right. I started an organization when I was just fifteen that none of you have heard of because it failed, and that's okay. My failure with that organization was the precursor to starting Zero Hour. So it all paid off.

THE FAILURE THAT LED TO THE SUCCESS THAT WAS ZERO HOUR

In the spring of 2017, in my freshman year of high school, I poured all my love, energy, blood, sweat, and tears into Future Voters for 350ppm. Yes, I am aware of how clunky and not-catchy the name is. Your girl was not well versed in communications or social media strategy at the time.

I had been lobbying in my state capital for climate justice for more than a year at that point with no legislative success. When I talked to my allies in the state legislature who wanted to pass the bills I lobbied for but couldn't convince their colleagues to, they all told me the same thing—all of the environmental lobbying was coming from activists in Seattle. The state representatives and senators cared about only their own constituents, and they hadn't received pressure to take climate action from people in their district. My representative told me that if I could get youth and adults from every district of Washington to consistently lobby and put pressure on their own representatives, the legislature would be more likely to budge.

So that's exactly what I set out to do. I had a single co-organizer, Chiara Rose D'Angelo, who was about twenty at the time and was known for her extreme and heroic environmental actions in the Pacific Northwest, like chaining herself to a Shell oil tanker for three days to stop it from setting sail to drill in the arctic.

Chiara and I made a plan to recruit two district captains in each Washington State local legislative district. The idea was to train two young people as leaders in each district to assemble an intergenerational lobbying team to regularly pressure their local state representative to vote on different climate action initiatives.

Our timeline was very ambitious—we were planning on recruiting all our district captains by the end of the summer, and then we were going to try to apply for grants, raise money, and train all our district captains by the end of fall. We called ourselves Future Voters for 350ppm because we wanted to make a point that even though most youth couldn't vote, we were still future voters, and that gave us power that our politicians couldn't ignore. The 350ppm stands for the 350 parts per million of carbon in the air that we need to get down to by the end of the century to survive the climate crisis.

Chiara and I spent a week building a website, creating social media profiles, and coming up with strategic messaging. Then Chiara and I got slammed with work outside of Future Voters. Chiara was buried in work with her other organization, Students for the Salish Sea, and all her work protecting Pacific Northwest orcas, and I had my hands full with a political summer program at Princeton University. It was around that time that the inspiration for a Youth Climate March—what later became Zero Hour—struck, and I started floating the idea of a youth climate march with my classmates at the summer program. Everyone was very enthusiastic, and I realized then that the necessary work of highlighting youth voices on the climate crisis didn't just need to happen in Washington State—it needed to happen nationally.

The tug in my heart to make the Youth Climate March happen was a lot stronger than launching Future Voters for 350ppm, which at that point was already starting to fall apart. No one wanted to be a district captain, but everyone was hyped about organizing the Youth Climate March. So I accepted that failure and focused my full energy on launching the march.

Zero Hour is not perfect at all. We have made tons of mistakes, we could fail on future projects and who knows? Someday we could cease to exist. But the point is we already succeeded in making an impact and meeting our original goal of creating a climate march led by young people internationally. Even if the organization disappears into thin air while you're reading this, the impact cannot be undone. We cannot un-march on Washington or un-lay the groundwork for the youth climate strike movement. The good has been done.

This is the bottom line: You don't have to get it right on the first try. You don't have to come from a wealthy or privileged background to start a movement. You don't have to have all the knowledge and resources from the get-go. If you have a strong vision, resilience, and a refusal to give in, you can make waves.

Take it from a normal teenager who built an international movement from nothing but a social media account with hardly any followers, an email account, and determination.

Pranjal Jain, Seventeen, She/Her
Rights of Indian women, immigration rights activist

JAMIE: How did you become an activist?

PRANJAL: I discovered I was an undocumented immigrant the same year Donald Trump was elected. I was fifteen years old and it was a huge shock to me. I always knew I was an immigrant, but I didn't know I was undocumented.

When I found out my immigration status, it changed everything. Before, I had lived my life like a regular American citizen.

I have been very privileged because I was able to become a naturalized citizen soon after I found out my status. I wanted to pay it forward.

I noticed there was a real need. There are many undocumented immigrants in my community who are now living in fear. It doesn't help that we are a community that is mostly people of color (POC), and the election helped to embolden white supremacists who feel they can attack us without consequence.

After seeing this spike of despair among fellow POC in my community, I decided to take action. I organized a post-2016-election healing event after school about the acceptance of people of all races, genders, and sexualities.

Since then I have organized events, campaigns, and projects working on different aspects of justice for the people I care about.

JAMIE: What are your strategies for creating change?

PRANJAL: I firmly believe we need to educate young people so that youth are equipped with the knowledge they need to be successful.

When I gave my menstrual equity workshop, none of my peers knew what it was about.

It was so scary. I was shaking. But because I was vulnerable, my peers understood. They opened up. My curriculum made my classmates see where they needed menstrual equity in their lives.

As a South Asian woman, the shame and taboo are so real with sexuality and menstruation, and I had to overcome my own culturally ingrained shame.

JAMIE: Why is it the little actions that can change the world?

PRANJAL: I believe in the grassroots. The nonprofit I am forming to empower and uplift women back in India is going to be one hundred percent grassroots change. Let's say my organization doesn't reach everyone—but even if I impact one family and get them to see the value in their females and send their daughters to school, it would be the best thing.

Bottom-up organizing is the only way real change happens.

5

GET CREATIVE—USING ART FOR A CAUSE

TAKING YOUR ACTIVISM FROM THE STREETS TO THE STUDIOS AND FROM THE STUDIOS TO THE STREETS.

It is a myth that you are an activist only if you are marching in the streets, visiting politicians' offices, leading protests, and giving powerful speeches. The way I look at it, the culture has to change first before the laws change. That is how it has always been. The government never goes ahead and makes a law freeing a group of people from oppression without a mass public and cultural outcry. Governments tend to be keen on maintaining the power structures and systems of oppression the way they are, and only when the culture has shifted so radically that they cannot get away with maintaining things the way they are do they change.

So if our goal is to shift the culture, we have to work on making influences in mediums that control the culture. So what does control our culture? Art. Music, photography, paintings, drawings, films, videos...if you think about what shapes and moves our society forward, it's art. If you think about what you spend most of your time listening to and looking at, whether an Instagram photo, a show, a song—all of that is art. So not only is it important to use art in our resistance and activism; it is vital. Because how else are we going to reach people? Art is a universal language, a way of making people see and understand experiences in a profound new light. Art influences society by changing opinions, instilling values, and translating experiences across space and time. Art is a way of taking up space and reclaiming narratives that are never told otherwise.

You as a singer, poet, writer, dancer, songwriter, musician, painter, cartoon artist, graffiti artist have a powerful tool in your hands to change the world. Every major justice movement has had an art component that helped drive the cause forward, motivate and give hope to the activists fighting for it, and bring those outside of the movement into it.

It's one thing to say, "According to a recent United Nations report, 1 million species are facing extinction," but it's a whole different dimension of powerful when that same fact is conveyed in a public mural that shows the percent of animals dying through graphic images. It's one thing to say, "Your policies on gun violence are killing children," but decorated Valentine's Day cards on politicians' desks that say, "You stole my heart—last year my brother was killed in a school shooting and you did nothing about it," are infinitely more hard hitting. (That was a real action taken by an organization called Change the Ref.) Art is a way to creatively display facts and messages to appeal to people's humanity and emotions and unlock something inside of them that makes them more receptive to your message. This strategy of artful activism is not simply making art that represents or discusses a cause; it incorporates artistic ways of strategically communicating hard-hitting messages.

One thing that young people bring to the table as change-makers is our creativity and ability to think outside of the box.

Instead of saying, "Millions of people are displaced by climate change every year," you can artistically and symbolically display it through visuals in front of your local government building.

WAYS TO USE YOUR SKILLS AS AN ARTIST TO MAKE CHANGE

1. **Incorporate art in actions and protests to make a powerful statement:** Politicians, media, business leaders, and the general public have seen people march in the street with signs a million times. So how do you better grab people's attention and create an action with a powerful message that will impact them on a deep level? Use art. Drop a large banner from a bridge with a message you want people in cars below to understand.

   During a fight to stop arctic drilling in the American Pacific Northwest and all over the world, banners with messages like "Save the Arctic" were dropped from cranes over shipping docks, creating incredible imagery of climate justice messages blocking or hanging over oil ships. Manuel Oliver, the father of Joaquin Oliver, a student who was murdered at Marjorie Stoneman Douglas High School in Parkland, Florida, in 2018 during a mass shooting, uses public art to highlight the trauma of everyday gun violence in America. He and his organization, Change the Ref, place disruptive art installations such as a rack of greeting cards with all the typical holidays paired with school shootings, making the point of how common shootings in the United States have become.

   Using light projectors on buildings at night can make awesome visuals for press and onlookers to take in. Let's say you want to find a creative way of exposing a bank for funding fossil fuel pipelines. On its building at night, you could project the words "sucks" or "kills our planet" or "funds polluters" under the big bank's logo. Because you're not actually physically damaging the property or painting on it, you should not be doing anything illegal. Light projection actions can be a creative way to make a bold statement.

Another great way to use artful activism is by setting a scene. I remember protesting the construction of a liquid natural gas terminal in Tacoma, Washington, with the Puyallup tribe, and the local organizers set up this whole graveyard scene right outside of the city council, dramatizing the point that continued fossil fuel extraction is killing our futures and that the city's approval of this new fossil fuel project would be a death sentence for our planet. Along with many other young people, we posed on the ground like corpses, and chalk outlines of our bodies were drawn on the concrete, like a crime scene. Then people set down fake tombstones beside us.

If you are just starting out and don't have access to a lot of resources, connections, or the capacity to organize an artistic action to the scale of the examples I used above—don't worry! You don't have to make your actions as big or as extreme. Chalk messages on a sidewalk can be effective as a starting point. In fact, make your protest or action a piece of art in itself. You don't have to stay within the constraints of what a traditional protest, action, or rally looks like. Movements are places to be just as creative as art studios.

This concept isn't just for the artists; it's for everyone organizing an action—if you start to compose your actions less like just putting together an event and more like creating a large work of art in itself, you're going to find yourself taking more powerful, bold, and out-of-the-box actions. You are not just an organizer anymore; you are a composer. Don't just say a statement—show the statement.

2. **Take up space that would never be given to you:** A lot of being a youth activist is about pulling the seat up to the table yourself, because no one is going to invite you. No one is going to open up space for our unique voices, stories, and concerns without us pushing for it. That's where street and urban art comes in. Reclaiming the streets for your people or your cause or just using the streets and public places to spread awareness, advertise events, and convey a message is a powerful form of activism in itself. Wheat pasting (a form of temporarily putting up signs, posters, art, and flyers in public) is illegal in some places but still used by many grassroots youth activists to generate momentum and a message for a cause.

    Research the rules for street art in your hometown. It's always important to know the codes where you live and how best to be safe and smart when doing any sort of urban art installation. Billboards and other planned, less-spontaneous and less-guerilla forms of public art are also extremely powerful.

3. **Make your protests and actions themselves a work of theater:** Visual art is not where the power of artistic expression to uplift a cause ends. There are totally ways for you to use theater, acting, music, instruments, and general performance art to do an amazing action and make a large impact. Flash mobs and public theatrical performances are also great ways to get a message across and generate interest and attention for a cause.

    Go to a very public area where there are going to be many people walking by to see your action. Bring speakers, costumes, and whatever else you need to stage your theatrical/musical action. It is best to also have people who are not performing standing on the side with signs and flyers with website information, social media handles, and sources of information about the cause if people are interested.

In most cases you will need a permit to do public art or performance, so you should check with your local government (it often takes nothing more than a quick internet search to find out about permitting laws where you live). It is important to know that if you just show up randomly somewhere and start to take up public space or cause some sort of scene, you will be met with resistance from the police or other institutions of authority. So be careful, plan ahead, and know exactly what the laws are wherever you are planning to perform.

An example of a performative action I took a few years back was a Seattle youth protest outside of a large coffee chain's headquarters, asking them to create a more sustainable and environmentally friendly cup, because the cups they were using had a massive wasteful footprint on the planet. This was around the winter holiday season, so we dressed up like the company logo and sang parody Christmas carols as the employees walked out of the headquarters, handing them flyers with the information about the environmental impact of their products. Behind us we had a giant "cup monster"—a sculpture made of plastic coffee cups dug out of the trash, representative of the number of cups thrown away every minute.

You see? The possibilities for bold artistic performance art actions are limitless. Get creative, be satirical, *go there,* and don't be afraid of being controversial and making people in authority upset. It is our job as young activists to point out when the emperor has no clothes, even when the rest of society goes along with the lie. Our power lies in our ability to call BS, speak truth to power, and expose the powerful for who they are. Art is an effective tool to point out the naked truth, and using whatever performing art skills you and the people you work with have, you can do just that.

It's time to think outside the box when approaching making change. The more bold, creative, inventive, daring, and out-there actions you take, the better. Make people cringe, gasp, cry, laugh—art evokes humanity and emotions. And in a world full of so much cover-up and logic that circumvents what really matters in our world, we need to cut right through and lay the raw, undeniable facts out...which is basically what art is. Peel away all the layers and just lay out the truth—no matter how hard it is for others to stomach. That is our job as young activists and as artists.

Sofya Wang, Twenty-One, She/Her
LGBTQ+ activist, queer Asian advocate, singer/
songwriter, multi-instrumentalist, actress

JAMIE: **Tell me about your music, videos, and the work
you do as an artist.**

SOFYA: I got started in music learning a bunch of
instruments as a kid. When I wasn't playing instruments,
I was singing in the shower. I wrote parodies and joke
songs at first, and then one day I thought, "What do I
actually want to do with my life if money isn't an issue?"
and it was singing. So I took production lessons and
started writing more music, and my first song was a
collaboration with my production teacher.

"Boys Aside" is the song/music video I am most
known for. It was actually my second song ever. I made
the video with my sister. We're indie, so we make
everything ourselves. I based the song and music
video off of this experience where I liked this girl.
Looking back, the music video and song is a character
I created. My new music is based on what I truly am
experiencing now.

JAMIE: **What has been your experience as a queer woman
of color in the music industry, and why is your art so
important?**

SOFYA: Art in general nowadays is people connecting with
authenticity. I'm just being me, and I happen to be an

Asian lesbian, so I understand that's much needed in the world to have representation. It's based on living life authentically.

JAMIE: **What have been the responses you've gotten online?**

SOFYA: I get a lot of messages from queer Asians asking me how I'm so comfortable. When they see themselves represented in me and my music, they feel more comfortable, or at least less alone. By living your life to the fullest and just being yourself, you can give other people permission to do so.

JAMIE: **What is your advice for people who want to start making a difference with their art and music?**

SOFYA: Focus on what's most important to you in your art, and everything will follow. Don't worry about the external. Ask questions along the way and figure out what's most important to you. If you authentically convey your message in art, people will gravitate to what you're making.

I know my causes are for LGBTQ+ rights, the environment, and education. It's easy to get caught up in day-to-day life, but I encourage you to hold on to a few causes and use your music to authentically amplify them.

THE ULTIMATE GUIDE TO EVENT AND ACTION ORGANIZING

FROM THROWING A FUNDRAISER, TO ORGANIZING A WALKOUT, TO MOBILIZING THOUSANDS OF PEOPLE . . .

Event organizing is often a major part of the job of being an activist. In some cases, you have all the time in the world to plan the most perfect and strategic action to convey your message just right. Oftentimes, events like summits and mass marches take a year or more of planning, coalition building (the process by which parties, individuals, organizations, or nations come together), and organizing to put on. But there are many cases where we are not afforded that luxury.

Let's say a shooting happens in a school. An unarmed Black person is shot by a cop. A fossil fuel pipeline is being built through your community. In these situations, an event has to be whipped together quickly. You don't have a year to craft the perfect messaging or speaker lineup—you just have to respond *now* to get people help or raise awareness.

Even in those very different circumstances, you can follow a general pattern. If you are rapid-response organizing, some of these steps might have to be skipped. If you are planning a long-term event for a movement, you can take your time and make sure each step is carefully executed.

So whether you want to host a small fundraiser, a summit, a conference, a community gardening event, a school walkout, a direct action, a strike, a launch party for an organization, or a national march on your country's capital, here is what you need to know about event and action organizing.

EVENT ORGANIZING 101

- **Identify the purpose, vision, and mission of the event/action:** Circle back to your *why*. Just open up a document on your computer along with the people who are working on the event with you and brainstorm. Type out the reasons why you are organizing the event, its purpose, and the mission of the action, and take some time to outline the vision of what you would like to happen that day (or days).

- **Set ambitious but realistic goals:** What is the goal of your action? What do you want the organizers and participants to get out of it, and how many people do you want to reach? How many people do you want to come? How much press do you want to generate on the topic you are organizing around? How many trees do you want to plant, people do you want to reach, and so on? Be ambitious, but also don't set yourself up for disappointment. Sure, I would have liked a million people to come to Zero Hour's Youth Climate March in Washington, DC, but that was not a realistic target. So we aimed for a few thousand and organized accordingly. With goal setting for an action or event, you have to find the happy balance somewhere between your grand visions and the reality of the resources at your disposal.

- **Identify what you don't know and who can fill in those gaps:** After you have an overall outline of what you want to do and why you want to do it, identify the gaps in your and your organizing team's knowledge. What needs to happen between now and the event that you don't know how to do or don't have the resources to do? Make a backward timeline—start from the event itself, and go backward, outlining everything that has to get done in order to get to that moment of a successful event. Whatever gaps you identify—for example, let's say no one on your team has any press connections or knowledge of how to work with the press—highlight them. Then focus on finding the right people to fill those gaps. Search around for the person you need to help you with press, or whatever it is that needs to be addressed, and fill all your gaps before moving full speed ahead.

- **Make a budget and fundraise:** Most things in this world cost money, and putting on an event is no exception. Although some actions, like an individual climate strike or school walkout, don't really take much funding, others—like a summit or mass mobilization—might require hundreds of thousands of dollars. Bring on an adult who has experience with nonprofit finance or even another young organizer who has done this before. It is important to know how much it is going to cost to put this action on and then actually raise that money. Your best bet for getting donations is crowdfunding—online sites like GoFundMe and Action Network are great platforms to set up and start raising cash.

- **Find a venue/location and apply for permitting if necessary:** Set the location for your event. If it is a march or rally, apply for a permit with the local parks department. A quick Google search on event permitting for public spaces can get you all the information you need.

If you are booking a space for your event, get on that right away. Venues tend to be booked far in advance, so compile a list of places within your price range, and start calling and emailing.

- **Plan out the day(s) and what will go down:** Plan out hour by hour the way the day or days will happen. It is important to make sure that you have every minute of your action planned out so when the day of the event comes, you know what lies ahead.

- **Invite speakers and presenters:** People don't like to be blindsided by an invite or request on short notice. Send speaker invitations as early as possible. Compile a list of those you want to make an appearance, speak, or present at your event; find their contact information; and start sending out emails and making phone calls. Then work with those speakers to make sure that they are on the same page with you about the vision of the event and how they will be contributing.

- **Make social media materials and promote:** Now it's time to announce to the world that your event is happening. (See Chapter 11 to learn about how to craft a social media plan and strategy for your event.)

- **Recruit attendees and participants:** Okay, time to make sure people actually show up! Spread the word in every way you can. Social media will not be enough. Give talks at community centers, hand out flyers, have one-on-one conversations with people and invite them to your event, send out emails, and make phone calls. Think about what it would take to get you to volunteer or attend an event despite your busy schedule, and do that! A recruitment plan should have a few main aspects to ensure turnout:
  - » Social media promotion
  - » On-the-ground organizing (knocking on doors to spread the word, handing out flyers)

» Word of mouth

» Email alerts

» Reminders to people who have said they are showing up

- **Write and send a press release:** If you are organizing something like a rally, summit, walkout, march, or protest that you believe is press-worthy, write up a press release and send it out to your press list the day before or the morning of the event. (For more on press and press strategy, see Chapter 10.)

THE DAY OF THE EVENT

- **Before the event starts, ground yourself and your team and run over the schedule:** Things can get hectic when you have a million and one things running through your mind as you are putting together an event. The morning before it starts, gather your fellow organizers and ground yourselves. It's easy to get caught up in the stress and emotion, so just take deep breaths together, remind yourselves of your goal and vision, and make sure to set the intentions and mood for the day. After you have grounded yourselves, run through the agenda one last time, and make sure everyone is on the same page.

- **Have safety measures in place and volunteers to coordinate the event and to make sure everything runs smoothly:** The bigger the event, the more security you're going to need. Have a good ratio of volunteers to attendees making sure that everything is running safely and smoothly. Have resources for people with chronic illnesses and disabilities and anyone who will need help and guidance during your event. Some events you put on are going to require professional security. The best way to find and hire security is to work with a trusted adult who has experience with putting on events and to research private security companies.

- **Have someone in charge of documenting the event:** If you are raising awareness about a cause, it's important to be in charge of your own narrative. Have someone in your inner circle in charge of taking photos and videos. Those photos and videos can be used for fundraising, follow-ups, press, social media, email alerts, and more.
- **Send a post-event press release and social media materials:** This only goes for large public demonstrations. If you are organizing an action where getting media attention is part of the strategy, it is important to send follow-ups as soon as possible after the event. Before you take a well-deserved nap after all your hard work, send out a follow-up email summarizing the event (along with photos) to the media you sent out the original press release to, and post pictures, footage, and takeaways from the event on social media.

AFTER THE EVENT

- **Rest and say *thank you:*** Take some time to rest, reflect, and decompress after the event. Send an email to everyone who attended your action thanking them for supporting the cause. Take the time to personally appreciate everyone on your organizing team who helped make the event happen. People work diligently to make events come to life, so make sure everyone who has put in effort is seen for what they have done.

  If you are in the midst of a series of rapid response actions, keep plugging ahead, but after the storm has passed, take some time for yourself. If you are organizing around a recent tragedy, take some time to feel and grieve. Give yourself permission to be not just an organizer and an activist but a person who has just been through something tough. As activists we are programmed to constantly react to things, but it's okay after spending so much time reacting, to just *be.*

The truth is, you never know the impact the event you (yes, YOU) organize could have, no matter how small and scrappy. Back in 2017 when I started Zero Hour, I felt alone, and I was skeptical any event I put on would move the needle on climate change.

Back when I was a scared fifteen-year-old trying to do my part to stop the climate crisis, youth climate activism was hardly recognized in the mainstream media or by leaders. I had no money, no notoriety, and yet the movement we young women in the United States started was a falling domino that helped lead to the mainstreaming of high school climate justice activism that you know today.

With nothing but determination and the internet, we organized the Youth Climate March and Youth Climate Lobby Day in Washington, DC, and twenty-five other cities around the world.

The day of the Youth Climate March, July 21, 2018, there was a rainstorm in DC. Everyone was drenched from head to toe, and at one point it looked like our scrappy operation was falling apart. Our cries for climate justice seemed like they were drowned in the storm.

But it turns out they weren't. The next day, we opened the Sunday *New York Times* to a full-page article covering our movement, spreading our message to the world.

Your low-budget march in the pouring rain could change the world. So get organizing! You never know what could happen.

Sara Jado, Eighteen, She/Her
Gun violence prevention activist, Sudanese rights and
Black Lives Matter activist

JAMIE: How did you become an activist?

SARA: I'm Black and Muslim. I didn't know my identities would affect me until I turned eleven. My teacher stopped and looked at me and all the students of color in the room and told us that "the world will be against you and you have to do everything you can to make it home to your parents. I don't ever want to see your face on the news as the unarmed Black kid who was gunned down. Speak up when you see injustice and speak up for kids like Trayvon Martin."

I was fourteen when I heard about the Chapel Hill shooting. I was so angry and devastated that Muslims were killed in their own homes. I started going to protests. On February 14, 2018, I was in my theater class, and heard about the deadliest school shooting in America's history [Parkland]. So I joined March for Our Lives and Black Lives Matter.

JAMIE: What are some of the most memorable moments of your activism?

SARA: On the *Road to Change* Greensboro tour stop, I wrote a speech about my struggles as a Black/Muslim organizer. After I gave that speech, the crowd's energy was wild. I knew I really impacted people that day.

JAMIE: What have been some difficult moments in your activism?

SARA: On August 12, eleven days after the *Road to Change* Greensboro stop, I lost my cousin in a shooting. I cried for days, and I got even more dedicated to fight against gun violence.

There are times I feel like I don't belong in a place that is majority white. Sometimes I feel like I cannot speak up or take up too much space, and sometimes I do feel tokenized working for an organization that is mostly white.

JAMIE: How do people help the causes you're fighting for?

SARA: In my community, people try to put in funding. People come out to events. On a national scale, nobody really cares about community shootings and local chapters in gun violence prevention.

JAMIE: What are your tips for other young activists who want to get involved?

SARA: If you think there's no space for you, yes, there is. If you don't feel safe in the organization, make your own space and platform. You do NOT need a big platform to make changes. Organizing isn't about the followers you get, it's about the change you make in your community. If someone tells you you're too loud, tell them, "Well you're not being loud enough about these issues."

BEING A YOUNG ACTIVIST—
WHAT'S THE SCOOP?

WHAT BEING A YOUNG ORGANIZER
IS REALLY LIKE.

Politicians always tell me, "Keep up the good work; your generation is going to save the world!"

They are both so right and so unbelievably wrong at the same time.

As young people, we do have great power to move the political needle toward change, and we have done it countless times in history before. But there are also many things not in our power, and it is unacceptable for leaders to put the burden of the problems they created and have the power to fix on our shoulders. Climate disaster is a perfect example of this. If we wait until Generation Z is old enough to be in power, it will be far too late to address this crisis. In fact, we are already deadly late on acting on the climate crisis. We do not have the full power to create and pass climate policy; we do not have the power to enforce laws or decide our countries' federal budgets.

We *do* have the power to influence those who have institutional power.

The key to being a successful young activist is to first understand the power you *do* have and the power you don't have. This is a basic breakdown of the unique power young activists hold in our society versus what is out of our control.

POWER YOUTH ACTIVISTS HOLD

- **Moral high ground:** Having the moral high ground is crucial when it comes to pushing public opinion and making leaders and corporations wake up to the issues. You didn't create the problem you're trying to solve, so your rage and organizing come from a genuine desire to make things better. This is true for young people when it comes to politics. No one can point to us and say, "Well you're just as responsible for climate change!" because no, we're not. We didn't create the systems of oppression that hold us down, and we are not old enough to be in the positions of power that enforce them. So when we speak, our message rings true because there is no hypocrisy in calling out our leaders. No one can point a finger back at us and say, "You're corrupt too!" because we're just kids trying to create a better world.
- **No special interests holding us back:** This is similar but not quite the same as holding the moral high ground. We the youth are not held back on what we can and can't say because of special interests. For example, many politicians are limited in what they can say and do and advocate for by the donors they rely on to get reelected.
- **Fresh energy and perspectives:** Youth bring new ideas to the table, as well as a fresh energy and drive that many of our elders have lost. No one knows better than we do what it is like

to grow up in the current time, and we are the most up to date when it comes to technology, pop culture, and having a finger on the pulse of mass culture.

- **Expertise on the issues that personally affect us:** Many adults in power do not comprehend or even hear much about important issues from young people's perspectives. They do not feel climate change like we do; they don't feel student loans or an economy that makes it increasingly difficult for us to find good-paying jobs like we do. When we speak about what we are going through, that rings true to people, and it looks bad for someone in power to discredit the lived experiences of a young person.

POWER YOUTH ACTIVISTS DO *NOT* HOLD

- **Legislative power:** We do not control any of the branches of government, local or federal, in any place in the world. We do not control what laws and policies are passed and instituted.
- **Monetary power:** We do not control the money of our world or have power in any large financial institutions. We do not control the banks, stock market, or large corporations.
- **Legal power:** We do not control the laws, police system, or how laws are enforced.
- **Institutional power:** We do not control businesses or bureaucracies.
- **Mainstream media power:** We do not control major news outlets that have millions of people watching them daily, and we cannot control the news cycle. We are not the executives in charge of major networks who get to decide what is covered and what is not.

So yeah...that's a lot we *don't* have control over. Which is why when it comes to instituting change, it's completely unfair for leaders to pin the blame on us. Our power lies in using what resources we do have to influence those systems.

Beyond knowing what power you do and don't have as a young person in this world, it is also important to know what you will be up against no matter what. Keep in mind that the more marginalized identities you carry, the more you will be up against. Know how the world perceives you (whether their perception is true or not) so you can best arm yourself to overcome their preconceived notions.

WHAT YOU AS A YOUTH ACTIVIST ARE UP AGAINST

- Patronizing and invalidation
- Lack of trust in your ability
- Systematic silencing of your voice
- Oftentimes, lack of funding and resources

HOW TO COMPENSATE FOR (WHAT THE WORLD PERCEIVES AS) YOUR WEAKNESSES

- **Know everything there is to know on your topic:** Many people are going to automatically assume that you as a young person don't know what you're talking about—which means you have to become an expert on your topic. Be overprepared.
- **Defy stereotypes and expectations of your immaturity and irresponsibility:** People may expect you to be impatient, immature, reckless, and rude. Be the most patient, mature, and polite person in the room.
- **Address the elephant in the room:** If someone is really testing your limits or being overtly rude or dismissive of you as a young person, don't be afraid to bring it up. Say, "If I were twenty years older and asking the same question, would you talk to me in the same way you're talking now?" The adult might get defensive, but just keep holding them accountable

for their behavior and pointing out the truth. Speak your truth to power! Always, always, always.

WHAT TO DO WHEN POWERFUL ADULTS DON'T TAKE YOU SERIOUSLY

- **Don't sink to their level:** In other words, be the adult in the situation. If an adult in power freaks out or says something stupid? Don't freak out back. Don't say something stupid back. Because when they do it, it's being "passionate." When you do it, it's being "an obnoxious teenager," being "a whiny little kid," or "throwing a temper tantrum." Is that a double standard? Totally. Is it fair? Absolutely not. But you have to play the game to win the game.

  Keep your long-term goals in mind, and pick your battles. Unsupportive adults will look for every opportunity to point at a young person being angry and emotional and say, *See, I told you the kids were like this!*

  There are some situations where you just gotta say, "Screw it," and do you. Freak out, get mad, yell when it's called for and appropriate and the issue is super serious. Use your best judgment. Being exactly what the world thinks you are— angry and loud—is just fine when you're calling out a politician in public for doing something horrific.

- **If appropriate, get footage so you can hold a poorly behaving adult publicly accountable:** This is more relevant with public figures such as heads of large companies or elected officials and bureaucrats. But if someone in power is being outwardly rude, condescending, inappropriate, or unreasonable and you have the opportunity post the interaction online to hold that public figure accountable, it could (in some cases) be a good call. In some cases, filming an interaction with a public figure is perfectly legal, like at a rally, press conference, or obviously public event—but there are some cases (like in a courtroom) where filming is not legal.

An example of this strategy working is when in 2019, a group of young climate justice activists asked a senator to sign a piece of environmental justice legislation called the Green New Deal (mainly focusing on creating a rapid transition away from fossil fuels and toward a renewable energy economy), and she responded in an extremely ageist, rude, condescending, and inappropriate way. This interaction was caught on video, and it went viral, holding the senator accountable for her treatment of young people as well as for ignoring the important issue of climate change. The senator was forced to release a statement responding to the resulting public outcry and promising to address the issue head on, leading to further dialogue.

I realize this chapter makes it sound like all adults are against you and you're going to be constantly swimming upstream and fighting to be heard—but that is not true. I warned you about what can go wrong, but there are so many adults out there who have your back. You will meet with elected officials and people in power who genuinely believe in you and the work you do and will want to do the best they can for whatever cause you are fighting for. You are not fighting against older generations. *Youth to Power* is not about generations sparring with each other; it's about knowing where your power lies and how to stand up for yourself when the powerful believe they can silence you. On your journey you will meet countless adults and people in power who will root for you and do everything they can to support you. Keep them close. You are not in this fight alone.

Zeena Abdulkarim, Eighteen, She/Her
Organizer for Zero Hour, intersectional feminist
fighting for social and environmental justice,
combating white supremacy

JAMIE: Tell me about the work you do and how you became an activist.

ZEENA: I did not have a choice other than to be an activist. I was raised in a very white town as a Black Muslim woman. Being a first-generation daughter of immigrants, I always had to fight and correct people on their ideologies of who my character and being was.

The main thing I had to make people understand was "Muslims aren't bad." People would tell me to go back to my own country; I was called a terrorist. There wasn't anything I could do other than educate them.

My step into being an organizer was when I was fifteen and felt very inspired from this outdoor academy where I was in the woods for four months. It brought to my attention that no one else was going to advocate for the things I needed. So I got involved with community organizing, working in a community center, working for the NAACP, and I started a social justice club.

In 2018 I organized a schoolwide walkout advocating for gun control. Then I organized a second one citywide. Soon after, I joined Zero Hour to fight for environmental justice.

JAMIE: What are the challenges you've faced?

ZEENA: People not taking me seriously.

Recently I realized the Black community doesn't accept me. I'm not Black enough to be friends with the Black kids or white enough with the white kids. I don't have generational history in America, so it's different from the Black American experience.

I've really struggled with imposter syndrome; I feel like I'm not doing enough. I feel like I'm not RIGHT for this work sometimes.

JAMIE: How do you overcome, and what advice do you have for young activists going through the same experience?

ZEENA: I realize this is a fight bigger than me. I am fighting for someone who can't fight for themselves. I am educating someone who needs educating.

My advice to youth is to be courageous, bold, and authentic. Say what you want to say. Educate yourself. Educate your mother, your brother, whoever. And especially for my fellow Black girls: I want you to know that you're heard, your stories and insight are valuable and precious. And not just Black girls but women of color everywhere. This is my love letter to you. I truly believe in Black girl magic; it's going to save the world.

8

PEACEFUL DIRECT ACTION

WHEN AN UNJUST LAW NEEDS TO BE BROKEN.

In the words of iconic civil rights leader Martin Luther King Jr., "One has a moral responsibility to disobey unjust laws....Protest beyond the law is not a departure from democracy; it is absolutely essential to it."

It is not always the same thing to be a good person and a good citizen. Some laws and norms like "polluting the planet and destroying all life on Earth is perfectly legal" and "it's not legal to be LGBTQ+" need to be challenged.

Challenging these laws and norms is called civil disobedience. Civil disobedience in a nutshell is the peaceful but active and public refusal of a citizen to obey certain laws that one deems unjust. It is often a last resort, when lobbying, negotiation, and other legal forms of action are not working. For example, with the issue of the climate crisis, more and more people are resorting to civil disobedience because for decades we have tried to negotiate, cooperate, and ask politicians and corporations nicely—without success. As the point of no return and inevitable human and planetary destruction looms nearer and more and more species go extinct and people die, the urgency rises to a new level.

Civil disobedience is a way of disrupting business as usual. To call it disrupting the peace is inaccurate. MLK best describes the necessity of civil disobedience in his famous "Letter from a Birmingham Jail," his response to white moderates criticizing Black civil rights leaders for resorting to civil disobedience. In this letter, King responds to a white moderate complaining about civil rights activists "disrupting the peace" by protesting segregation with civil disobedience. White moderates agreed with the goal of ending segregation, but they were uncomfortable with the noise and disruption and thought protesters should work in a less disruptive way. King responds that there is no peace in a society where the violence of racism exists.

The "peace" that civil rights protesters disrupted was not a positive one. It was what MLK called a "negative peace." Civil rights protesters didn't cause any violence. King explained that all they did was bring forward the ugliness of the violence that Black people in America face every day. They did not disrupt the peace; they just brought to the public's attention that there was never any peace to begin with.

There still exists a negative peace in our society. You may not see violence obviously manifested in the form of daily riots, but the violence exists in the everyday injustices that go unaddressed. Consider the daily violence of homophobia that queer people endure. Maybe knives aren't being pulled out, but the everyday denial of basic human rights, dignity, representation, and equal treatment by our cis straight counterparts is violence. The epidemic of homeless LGBTQ+ youth? That is violence because it causes harm.

That's why it's inaccurate to say that environmental protests are "disturbing the peace." There never was peace to begin with!

Allowing corporations to destroy all life on earth is not peace. The activists are simply bringing that quiet violence into the light, where people can no longer ignore it.

Beyond the civil rights movement, direct action has been used in recent movements for change. Most notably in the environmental movement, direct action has been wildly successful, especially in the Pacific Northwest, where I live and fight. The Shell No campaign to stop the corporation from drilling for oil in the Arctic was successful in stopping the fossil fuel company from Arctic drilling for that expedition. Kayaktivists blocked the ships from leaving port to go drill. That's right, a line of people in kayaks physically barricaded the ship. A lot of those people who put their bodies on the line to stop the oil tanker were youth. My friend Chiara Rose chained herself to an Arctic oil drilling ship when she was nineteen years old for three days, with a sign that said "Save the Arctic." Her act of civil disobedience, along with the kayaktivism and other creative forms of nonviolent direct action, successfully stopped Shell Oil.

The Extinction Rebellion in Europe is seeing activists glue themselves to important places of politics and business to protest the sixth mass extinction of plant and animal species on planet Earth that climate change is causing.

The Standing Rock #NODAPL movement held off the construction of the Dakota Access Pipeline for almost a whole year because indigenous youth organized members of the entire global Native community to physically stand in the way of the construction of the pipeline.

I am using examples from the climate justice movement, but civil disobedience is being used in every cause you can think of, from reproductive rights to the appointment of controversial government officials to racial justice to LGBTQ+ rights.

The most notable act of youth civil disobedience was the Children's March in the 1960s, in Birmingham, Alabama, demanding an end to segregation. When the civil rights movement was at a low point and some leaders were beginning to lose hope, Black children in this highly segregated town walked out of school by the thousands and marched in the streets, peacefully demanding an end to segregation. Because the children flooded the streets of the city without a permit (disrupting business as usual), police unleashed dogs and massive power hoses on them. They were thrown in jail by the hundreds. Soon the jails were filled with young children, and authorities didn't know what to do.

As soon as they were released from jail, the youth walked out of school again and into the streets and were arrested again and again. The power of the Black youth in Birmingham was felt all over the United States. The media covered it, and the activists who took part in it spoke to the press. Images of the protest were in newspapers all over the country, and footage was broadcast to everyone's living room TV screen.

Seeing children peacefully marching out of school for justice in their community being met with such cruelty by authorities moved the conscience of the country. The injustices that had been hidden for so long were brought to light in an obvious and ugly way. The negative peace was disturbed, and the racist power structure could no longer be ignored.

After the children's marches, the civil rights movement was reinvigorated, and President John F. Kennedy moved swiftly to push for the end of segregation in the United States once and for all.

It was the bravery of the student activists—some as young as six years old—that moved the conscience of a country and brought an end to a dark period of racist Jim Crow laws that had plagued the United States for more than a century.

If civil disobedience is something you want to get involved with, here are the basics.

CIVIL DISOBEDIENCE FOR YOUTH 101

- **Identify your privilege and risk levels, as well as your boundaries:** Before you put yourself in a vulnerable position, make sure you take some time to mentally prepare and set boundaries. What are you willing and not willing to do? Are you willing to risk arrest? Are you comfortable handling hate or potential aggression from police and counter protesters?

  Get out a piece of paper and make two columns. One that says, "I am willing to" and one that says, "I will not," and write down all of the potential scenarios and activities in direct action and civil disobedience that you would and wouldn't be okay participating in.

  Once you have taken some time to really be with yourself and see what you are and are not comfortable with, let everyone around you who is participating in that action know your boundaries, and make sure they respect them, so organizers know what tasks to give and to not give you, and what situations you are and are not okay being put in. Before an action, you also need to assess your own privilege levels. This is not about who you are but about how the world perceives people like you and what risks you may run into. For example, if you are a person of color, especially a young Black or Hispanic person, you are at a much greater risk of being targeted and profiled and experiencing violence during an action than if you are a young white person. According to the NAACP, African Americans are incarcerated at more than five times the rate of white people for the same crimes.

  So research and think about the visible identities you carry—your race, skin color, ethnicity, symbols of faith (like a hijab), queerness, and other outwardly recognizable factors of your identity. Think about how the world sees you: even if the perception of you at first glance is not all that you are, it is what law enforcement will see. You have to be extremely aware of how you would be perceived by a police officer. Think about the unfortunate societal risks and dangers that come with whatever identity you are—as unfair and uncomfortable as it is to acknowledge, it is important to keep in the back of your mind.

Every country has different stereotypes and prejudices of different ethnic groups, so in whatever country you're practicing civil disobedience, keep those in mind, and where you and those doing the action with you fit in. I say this because your safety comes first, always. No action is worth risking your life for. You have to be alive to continue the fight.

Also be aware of how your identity might privilege you during an act of civil disobedience. You can take advantage of it to be a more strategic ally/accomplice.

If you have privilege, use it to put yourself on the line on behalf of your less privileged siblings in the movement. If you are of an identity that is profiled and targeted, some actions might be safer for you to work on behind the scenes and not directly put your body on the line. The reality is horrifying and so unfair, but until we completely dismantle all systems of oppression, we have to be strategic about who is doing what in an act of civil disobedience so everyone stays safe.

- **Know the law:** If you are going to commit an act of civil disobedience, it is important to know what laws you are breaking and what the consequences are. You need to know exactly what you'll be getting yourself into.
- **Discuss the action with your parents/guardians:** I would *not* at all advise breaking the law or doing a risky direct action without telling your parents or guardians. This is a must if you are a minor, and even if you are not a minor, it would be better if your immediate family is well briefed about what

you're doing. It may be hard to convince your parents to let you do the action, so I would sit them down well ahead of time and have an honest conversation about why it is important and how they can make sure you are safe while participating. You can tell them how safe it will be and the details of the action, and maybe even have your parents with you during the action—but if they say no, I wouldn't advise sneaking out or going behind their back. Have someone else in your organization be the one who does the physical action, and you can take a more behind-the-scenes role.

- **Join an organization, form a coalition, and connect with experienced mentors:** Some solo acts of civil disobedience have changed the world. A friend of mine and sister in the climate justice movement, Greta Thunberg, a young white girl, performed a single-person school strike outside of the Swedish parliament in 2018 for climate action. She was fifteen. That single act of civil disobedience had a massive impact all over the world. She was in a country that is pretty safe and protective of people's right to protest, and she did not actively block or disrupt anything. She is also a white girl, and when it comes to police brutality, white women tend to receive preferential treatment by law enforcement and are the least profiled and targeted.

  With a nondisruptive action like a school strike in a relatively safe area, doing an action alone as a young white person is generally safe. But when it comes to doing an action in a country that has a tendency to crack down on protesters and when you are actively getting in the way of something, say, physically stopping traffic or construction, or when you carry many marginalized identities, it is very unsafe and ineffective to be alone.

  As a young person doing a high-risk action, you need a large team of people who can keep each other safe, preferably with some civil disobedience veterans who have participated in actions like this before. It is important to have a team that understands all the members' strengths and weaknesses, has diverse skill levels, and knows how to keep each other safe. Not only is it so much safer, but larger numbers make the action a lot more effective. Plus, having a community doing the action with you makes it so much more fun and joyful!

- **Have direct asks and reasons for your action:** If you are going to engage in nonviolent direct action, you need to have concrete asks of whoever you are protesting. It can't be something vague like "racial justice" or "reproductive rights"—it needs to be a tangible action. The point of a direct action is to apply pressure for a change to be made—but you have to specify what exact change it is that you want! Examples of concrete demands are stopping a construction project, keeping a local abortion clinic open, passing a law, complying with a treaty. Spoon-feed the authority you are demonstrating the solution you want, so that they have no excuse to say that they don't know how to proceed.

- **Plan for everything that could go wrong:** You need to be prepared for what to do if counter protesters show up, police start being aggressive, and other scenarios. Just like you would always rehearse a play before performing it, you have to run through the action with the group of people you are planning to do it with and prepare your reactions to different eventualities.

Rehearsing how the action will go down is always a good idea, and it's important in those trainings that everyone talk about what to do in every possible scenario. The group of people you are doing the action with should be united and all on the same page—nothing kills the effectiveness of an action like division and conflict within your own team. You cannot control what other people will do, but you can control your team's reaction to them, and *that* is what you need to have on point. Planning ahead of time means that if things get tense, you won't panic and get confused, because you have prepared a peaceful response.

- **Remain peaceful:** No matter what, civil disobedience does not work if you resort to violence. The number one rule in any direct action is to remain peaceful. Martin Luther King Jr. put it this way: "Nonviolence is a powerful and just weapon which cuts without wounding and ennobles the man who wields it. It is a sword that heals."

  If your action turns violent, it loses its power because the whole point of these actions is to arouse the conscience of a society. If you are fighting, the media and politicians can easily spin coverage to make it look like you are the aggressor. So not only is remaining peaceful crucial for your own safety during the action; it is crucial for the effectiveness of the action so the public is properly impacted. No matter how hostile and violent authorities or counter protesters become, if you remain loving and peaceful, you are going to impress the public and inspire their support. The authorities end up looking bad by being the violent ones while the protesters retain the moral high ground.

When young people break unjust laws peacefully, a society is forced to think, *Why would the kids put themselves on the line like that?*

Malia Hulleman, Twenty-Four, She/Her
Earth Defender, Water Protector, food justice
activist, indigenous justice activist, Kanaka Maoli
(indigenous Hawaiian)

JAMIE: How did you become an activist?

MALIA: I was born and raised in Hawaii. It's different being indigenous Hawaiian than being indigenous to Turtle Island (the United States mainland). We're the majority. We grow up with our own culture and language. Still, so many things have been lost because of colonization. Colonized Hawaii is a by-product of corporate greed. When you realize that, you start not wanting to say you are American. Hawaiian rights inspired me to stand up for our right as a sovereign people.

JAMIE: When did you get invested in being an Earth Defender and a Water Protector?

MALIA: Mauna Kea is the most sacred mountain to our people.

Because Hawaii is the most geographically isolated place in the world, there is hardly any light pollution, which makes it a great place to study the stars. Six or seven countries wanted to create a *massive* telescope.

We indigenous Hawaiians are the original astronomers! But Mauna Kea is a delicate ecosystem with endangered species.

Telescopes produce large amounts of chemical waste. That waste is stored in underground vats, which leak into the soil.

That's why my community is taking direct action to protect Mauna Kea and prevent construction on it, including camping on the mountain even though it is cold and the air on the top of the mountain is very thin.

JAMIE: What pushed you to join the Standing Rock #NODAPL movement?

MALIA: I was in the film industry in Los Angeles. I had decided to move there to pursue film.

When I was there, my friend told me about Standing Rock, about the pipeline and the kids running to raise awareness.

So I organized a caravan to go to the 2016 Democratic National Convention. The original Standing Rock youth protesters, who were running from their reservation across the country to raise awareness about the pipeline, were in Ohio. I met up with them there, and we organized rallies together.

On my way to New York with the Standing Rock runners, we got word that pipeline construction was starting. So we headed there to protect the water and stop the pipeline. Now with the telescope situation on Mauna Kea, I am fighting again to defend indigenous land.

JAMIE: What are your tips for young activists?

MALIA: As protectors, we become hardened. If you keep moving fast, you're going to become depressed and BURN OUT.

My elders tell me they've been taking it day by day.

You do not have to fight for every cause. You do not have to fight alone.

Encourage others to be leaders.

Most of the time the solutions are in the little things we do.

9

POLITICIANS, CONGRESS, AND LOBBYING, OH MY!

MAKING YOUR VOICE HEARD IN OUR POLITICAL INSTITUTIONS.

The government is supposed to work for the governed. No matter where in the world you live, your government is supposed to serve you and your best interest. Their job is to look out for you, not themselves—but often they forget.

Let's get into what exactly lobbying is, how it works, why it's important that youth lobby, and how you can become a lobbying pro!

LOBBYING AS A YOUNG PERSON 101
What Is Lobbying?

Lobbying is the act of attempting to influence the actions, policies, or decisions of politicians. If you boil down what politics is, it is the fight for control of the political agenda. It is vying for your concerns and needs to be considered in the public conversation and then translated into public policy. Lobbying is seeking to influence a politician or public official on an issue. This can be done in many ways, like calling your political representative's office, setting up meetings, engaging in other forms of discourse, and applying political pressure. Just because you can't vote, just because you are not an employed member of government or don't hold a position of power, does not mean you can't influence the political agenda.

Lobbying is usually only effective in democracies, because the power behind it is all about making politicians understand their constituents (the people who voted them into office) care about an issue. Elected officials are constantly worried about keeping their job and winning their next election. So if enough constituents make it clear that they feel very strongly about an issue (for example, passing a Green New Deal), their elected officials will realize that unless they support their cause, they will be voted out of office.

In democracies, lobbying is what bridges the gap between what you need and what your elected officials do in their seat of power. The United States is a representative democracy, which means we the people elect politicians to vote on bills on our behalf. When politicians don't hear from their constituents, they are less likely to vote for and work toward initiatives that actually help us. Lobbying is a way of reminding elected officials who they are really supposed to work for and reeling them back in to your needs.

Why Should Young People Lobby?

Let's say that you alone have the power to choose what TV show you and your family watch every night for a year. This is a big decision that's going to have a long-lasting impact, so everyone in your family will try to convince you to pick the show they want to watch. It's not exactly a fair decision, because some members of your family are more powerful and have much better access to you than others. Your brothers and sisters are off at school all the time, and they don't have much to offer you in return. They make up the majority of the population of your household, but because they have so much to do, have hardly any resources, and spend so much time away from you, they don't really get the chance to make the case for their favorite show. However, your rich uncles have all the time in the world to spend with you. They make their case to you for their favorite show, make promises in return for choosing their show, and take you out to fancy restaurants and make you feel doted on and special. They make up a very small percentage of your household population, and their preference in TV show does not reflect the preference of the majority of your family, but they have the biggest influence on you.

So by now you can guess that in this scenario you are the politician. Your powerless siblings are the constituents, the common people who make up the majority of a country's population but don't get to spend a lot of time with their representatives. The rich, charismatic uncles are the professional lobbyists for big corporations and special interests. They have the resources to pamper the politicians and influence them.

This is what we're up against. Even though the vast majority of the population does not have the same interests as professional lobbyists for big corporations, the ones who have the most access to our decision makers. The ones whispering in the politicians' ears are Big Pharma (pharmaceuticals), Big Oil, Big Agra (farming), and corporations that are often the main cause of the issues we're fighting against, like climate change. This gets worse and worse the higher level of government you go, so what we find in politics is a large disconnect between what politicians are encouraged to do and what the people they work for (us!) actually need them to do. Because representatives (in theory) do work for *us*—the people. At least in democracies, we the people vote them into power. Despite having money, corporations don't have a vote, and this is what we the people have going for us.

If you are not already a voter, you are a future voter. If you are in an immigration situation or another hard place where you will not be given your right to vote any time soon, you have influence over voters around you. Children have more influence on their parents than anyone else, and those politicians need your parents' votes.

You have the power to make your community's needs and your generation's needs heard and considered by your government. Setting up a meeting with your elected officials is a way of asserting your voice and your needs. Lobbying elected officials as young people makes our leaders face the next generation they work for, even though we haven't voted them into office.

Don't let the fact that you are under voting age, undocumented, or disenfranchised in another way make you feel like they don't owe you anything. You can even say right to an elected official's face, *I am a future voter, XYZ year will be my first voting election, my family has voted you in office for years, but we will not vote to reelect you unless you . . .*

Who Do You Lobby?

You're pumped and ready to make your voice heard in the political system! You have an issue you really care about and something you need elected officials to do or to stop doing. Now how do you actually reach them, and who exactly do you talk to?

In the United States, there are many levels of local and federal governance. You have your town or city's local council or government, which makes laws specific to your city or town; there is your state government, which makes laws that apply only to your state; and then there's the national government, which makes laws that apply to everyone in the whole country. The more locally you lobby, the better chance you have of getting something through a government body. The higher up in ranks of government you go, the more obstacles there are to pass a law or get something done.

This does not mean you shouldn't lobby your national government—this just means that often you can be most effective at the local level. But your voice is needed everywhere, so you can lobby at all levels accessible to you. There is nothing holding you back.

So how do you contact your representatives and set up a meeting with them? Well, with the internet, it is extremely easy. If you don't know who your senator or congressperson is (and again, my expertise is in the US political system), just google something like, "What is the legislative district of XYZ city?" Your legislative district will come up. You can also look up, "Who is the congressperson for XYZ town?" or "Who are the senators of XYZ state?" From there, you can just search that representative's name to find their website or the website of your state legislature. On that website there will be an email and phone number for constituents to call.

If you simply want to let your representative know how you feel and what you need but you don't have the time to set up an in-person meeting, just call that number. Actual elected officials won't pick up the phone, but their assistants and legislative aides will, and you can tell them what you wanted to tell your representative. It's as easy as, *Hi, my name is Jamie, I am a constituent of Senator Governmentperson, and I am calling because I oppose the construction of the natural gas plant and I need the senator to do everything in her power to stop it from being built. It is going to have a horrible effect on my health and the health of my whole community if it is constructed. I will be of voting age in this upcoming election, and my parents have voted for Senator Governmentperson every election she ran, so I hope to be able to support her. But if she lets this new project go through, my family will be very hurt and will not be able to support her anymore.*

The aide will always tell you they will relay the message to the representative. They tally how many constituents call about an issue, so if many people called opposing that natural gas plant, the aide would tell the senator that it is a matter of great concern to her constituents. Oftentimes, especially in local government settings, the people who pick up the phone are the elected official's legislative aides—the same people who help draft policy. So don't be disappointed because the elected official didn't come to the phone—often it's their staff that has the best ability to respond to you.

If calling is not your style, you can send a good old-fashioned paper letter. I say letter instead of email because so many organizations have automatic email programs that flood representatives' inboxes, so email is the worst way to reach a representative. A paper letter will be received a lot better and will actually be read by the office, if not the elected official themselves.

So now what do you do when you actually want to have a face-to-face meeting with an elected official? Oftentimes, this is the most effective way to reach them. In a face-to-face meeting, you can communicate what you need in a more personal way. On a local government website or the elected official's website, you can find the phone number and email of their staffers, and you can send them an email to set up a meeting. Simply say in the phone call and email that you are a constituent and you would like to meet with the elected official, and give some times that work best for you. Especially when it comes to local government, the aides are pretty responsive and will help you get a meeting. Meetings with constituents are common. Just like corporate Big

Oil special interest lobbyists have the right to set up a bunch of meetings with members of government, so do you!

What Lobbying Looks Like for You

So you scheduled a meeting with your representative or your representative's aide. (Sometimes the politician themselves can't have a meeting, but it's still great for you to meet with their staff. They are the ones who draft the policy anyway.) It's time to get in there and live out the true meaning of democracy. It's time to infiltrate the power structure and make sure your needs are recognized in the political system too. So how do you prepare, and what do you do when you get to the meeting?

THE DOS OF LOBBYING

- **Go with a group:** Lobbying is most effective when you have a team to do it with you. Oftentimes, organizations will schedule lobby days when many members go to speak to representatives. If you are not a part of an organization, that is fine. Gather a group of friends who believe in what you will be advocating to go with you.

  There is power in numbers. First of all, it will be a lot less nerve wracking for you if you have a support system, and also the whole point of lobbying is to make an elected official aware of what their constituents care about—so the more people in the room, the more they realize how much people care about this issue.

- **Prepare what everyone will say ahead of time:** The bigger the group going with you to lobby, the more you have to prepare and make sure everyone is on the same page. Elected officials are very busy people with tons of meetings and scheduled bill votes, so on average you're only going to get five to fifteen minutes with them.

If you're meeting with a staff person, you're going to get more quality time for discussion. No matter what though, delegate who in the group is going to say what. Maybe one person introduces the group, another brings up the issue, another tells a personal story relating to the issue, and another wraps up the conversation and hands out the follow-up materials.

- **Tell a story:** Facts are not what move most people to change— stories are. When was the last time someone showed you a chart or a fact sheet that sparked emotion in you, captivated you, and gave you a deep desire to change? For most people, it's never. But I'm sure everyone can remember a time when someone told you a story that changed the way you viewed something, maybe even how you viewed the world. Stories are a universal way of communicating and connecting with each other on a deep emotional level. If someone said, "Hey want to hear me read a list of facts?" you would most likely say, "No thanks" (at least I would!). But if someone says, "Want to hear a story?" you're going to be more interested.

Everyone has a story, often many, and there are stories behind every issue, bill, and initiative. Sure, maybe there are a lot of facts about climate change that your legislator needs to hear, and by all means make them aware. But remember: politicians are people, and people are moved by stories. So have someone who has been personally affected by the climate crisis tell a story about how they have been hurt and what it has done to them. If you are lobbying about reproductive rights, have someone tell a story about how access to reproductive health care has helped them and what their lives would look like if they didn't have it. You are painting a picture for the elected official or their staff about the actual lives that are being affected behind the issue. Politics is personal. Politics affects lives, and policy can fix or destroy lives—don't let them lose sight of that. Tell a story.

- **Be polite, pleasant, and civil:** Even if you are talking to a politician who is really hostile to your cause, be polite. You can disagree and call them out in a civil way that will not burn any bridges. The goal is not to get blacklisted from a politician's office; the goal is to start a dialogue and make them listen to you. If someone was yelling at you and calling you names, you would not give them the time of day or consider their side of things.

- **Follow up:** This meeting was just the beginning of your conversation. One meeting does not change policy, but consistent relationship building, persuasion, and advocacy does. So get the legislative staffer's contact info, and send a follow-up email! The sooner after the meeting, the better. Politicians meet with so many people, it's not personal if they don't remember you, so you want to hit them with that follow-up while you're still fresh in their minds. Write a follow-up email to the staffers, thank them for their time, attach any information that you want them to look over, and talk about next steps.

- **Get a picture with the politician:** It is always a good idea to get a picture with the politician you're lobbying and post about your meeting and what you discussed online. Tag the politician's social media in your post. Their staff might see it, and that's another way to stay in their minds. Also, this starts a conversation with your peers, showing them that you, a young person, can participate in democracy, and it makes meeting with representatives less foreign and scary for your friends and those who follow you. It is also a way of applying public pressure. Post something like, *We just had a meeting with Senator Governmentperson about the Green New Deal. We hope she listens to the youth and takes urgent climate action now before it is too late by voting for this bill. My family will not vote for her* *reelection if she does not protect our planet and our lives and futures.* That puts your conversation out in public and is another added pressure that applies the heat to your ask.

THE DON'TS OF LOBBYING

- **Don't hand your representative any written materials before or during the meeting:** This is a common rookie mistake. Most of the time, elected officials and staff members try to be attentive during meetings. They work for you, after all. You are their employers, never forget that! So if you hand them a fact sheet, a petition, or any other materials before the meeting is over, they will try to read what you gave them while listening to you at the same time, and they won't give you their full attention. If you have any written materials, give them after the meeting is over. You need their full eyes and ears, especially when it comes to storytelling and connecting with them on an emotional level, which is always most effective.

- **Don't be rude, unpleasant, or uncivil (don't burn bridges!):** This is self-explanatory. Don't make unnecessary enemies.

- **Don't talk about many different issues during the meeting:** Don't bring up a bunch of unrelated issues during one meeting. Keep the meeting targeted and focused on one—*one*—main ask. It's going to take you the full meeting to make a good case about one issue, and bringing up a bunch of different topics scatters the meeting, makes your message way less powerful, and leaves the elected official with no one main takeaway.

- **Don't let yourself get distracted or put off track:** This is especially true if you are a young person. Elected officials might try to play nice with you and ask all about school and other things that have nothing to do with the issue at hand. I've had elected officials talk really condescendingly to me about my life and school, purposely trying to use up the limited time we had, distracting me from making my case. Oftentimes, this isn't malicious—sometimes an elected official will be really happy to see a young person in their office and want to make small talk. A little small talk is always good; you have to be friendly and build a relationship, but keep in mind that you have limited time and you are there for a reason. No matter what the politician tries to twist, always spin back to the original goal of the meeting, and stay on track no matter what.

- **Film the meeting:** Elected officials have cameras thrust at them a lot, and when something is being filmed, they have a tendency to act for the cameras. Your goal is to have an honest human-to-human conversation with an elected official, and filming it takes the personal touch away and makes it feel like you are trying to put them on the spot. If a politician knows they're being filmed, they will be less likely to genuinely open up to you and won't share with you anything off the record that they do not want made public yet. If you film something, it could be posted anywhere or leaked to press, and elected officials don't want that. Your goal is to make a connection and be persuasive, and filming the meeting takes that aspect of trust away.

No matter what, just keep at it. Lobbying is all about applying pressure and keeping the pressure there. Don't get discouraged. One meeting is not going to change everything. But everything adds up. Your important conversation with an elected official stacks onto another person who just talked to them about the same subject, and that keeps your issue in the politician's mind. You never know whether your story, your conversation, your initiative, will be the one to tip the scale and make change happen. Keep the pressure on, keep the heat on, and don't ever let them forget you and your power!

Hadiya Afzal, Nineteen, She/Her
Youth civic engagement activist, ran for DuPage
County Board in Chicago

JAMIE: How did you decide to run for office when you were seventeen?

HADIYA: As a Muslim American, the election of Donald Trump was devastating. I spent months in a funk and was motivated to go to the Women's March on Washington. When I saw that energized activist space, I thought, *Okay the world didn't end. There's still a fighting spirit.*

I started attending county board meetings, where I saw the total lack of representation. Even though my community has a growing number of immigrants and a large Hispanic population, none of those groups were represented, plus there were no young people.

The budget is the biggest thing the county does. At the end of the day, *a budget is a moral document* and reflects the priorities of the board and town. If there are no young people, immigrants, people of color, and only four women advocating for what is in the budget—what does that say about the priorities laid out?

The county was looking for people to run in my district. The minority communities had no representation. I wanted to change that.

JAMIE: **What's it like running for office as a teenager?**

HADIYA: You're forced to know your truths. Issues, motivations, policies, people you want to speak to.

As a seventeen-year-old knocking on doors with my baby face asking people to vote for me, I had to spit some FACTS, or else people were going to dismiss me.

JAMIE: **What's your advice for other young people who want to run for local elected office?**

HADIYA: Get involved in your local party. Make connections with activist groups. Oftentimes there's a rift between grassroots and political parties—be the link. You have to make sure you serve everyone in your area. But please, never canvass alone! Cultivate openness, transparency, and feedback within your team. Make sure the campaign team understands everyone else's needs and boundaries. Make hard asks on the phone or in person—without fundraising, it is impossible to run. You aren't asking for someone to give you money to spend. You are asking them to place their faith in the campaign. Donating to a campaign is like voting, but early.

When it comes to running for local office, it will *never* get easier. You will become more experienced, but it will always be hard, stressful, and you will always be adapting.

The only way all that grueling work is worth it is if you're centered on the motivations of your campaign.

10

DON'T LIKE THE NEWS?
BECOME THE NEWS.

EVERYTHING YOU NEED TO KNOW ABOUT THE PRESS AND HOW TO WORK IT TO YOUR ADVANTAGE.

If you see an issue you care about in the media, taking action changes the news story. So the story is no longer *the climate crisis is here and it's terrifying* but *the climate crisis is here and young people are fighting back.*

The media—newspapers, magazines, TV shows, radio shows, blogs, online videos, and whatnot—shape the cultural narrative, the stories we tell, and the way we perceive the world around us. Oftentimes, what we see when we turn on the TV are politicians, CEOs, political analysts, and other "experts" speaking about the issues they care about from their own perspectives. Even though young people make up a huge percentage of the global population and of each country, the issues that matter to us are hardly ever covered on mainstream news channels and publications—up until very recently, when young activists began harnessing the power of media to shed light on our lived experiences.

Press is not the end goal of a movement—however, using it is a powerful strategy to achieve an end goal. For example, if your movement is all about LGBTQ+ rights and liberties in your country, getting press in itself will not end the discrimination. But getting press will spread awareness about the issue, and if communicated correctly, it can change minds and help change the culture in the right direction.

Getting your protest, campaign, action, rally, speech, or cause in the press is a great way of amplifying your message to a much wider audience and exponentially increasing your impact. So how do you get in the media? How do you get the news crews to come to your event? How to you get an article written up about the work you are doing?

HOW TO CREATE A MEDIA STRATEGY 101

- **Bring on the right people:** Before jumping in and learning how to do all the press outreach yourself, contact people on social media, via email, or in your own community who have experience working with the media. It is always a big advantage to have at least one adult mentor who knows the press basics and beyond on your side—they can help prevent you from making rookie mistakes and help you build long-term relationships with reporters.

  I'm going to be honest: getting press to cover you is all about relationships. Building solid relationships with reporters is very helpful when you need someone to cover your action or campaign, and having someone in your corner who has these connections and relationships makes a world of difference.

  So how do you find a media mentor? When you email different organizations, make calls, or even post on social media, you can say something like, *I'm a young activist organizing XYZ movement, and we need someone with press experience to help guide us through the process. Please direct message me if you are or know someone who can help out.*

How I did it: Before the 2018 Youth Climate March, I went to several environmental conferences and grassroots organizing trainings, and in these spaces I made it absolutely clear that my team was made up of a bunch of high school students who didn't know the first thing about media strategy and we needed help. Several people at one of the conferences said they personally weren't press experts but they might have some connections. And sure enough, one day over the phone, I was looped in to a woman named Shravya, from an organization called Climate Nexus, which focuses on getting climate in the media. She saved Zero Hour's butts for the 2018 Youth Climate March when it came to press strategy. Shravya came onto our team and was willing to volunteer her time and energy to help get our organization coverage in the press.

Know that what you usually need is not a publicist but a PR mentor whose first priority is your movement. A publicist is someone who pushes a person or issue out into the media as much as possible. A PR mentor puts the good of the movement over just trying to make you famous. Shravya would tell me if I was being too egotistical and press oriented, and even though she helped Zero Hour get coverage, she also kept us grounded and humble and let us know when press wasn't necessary. You need a movement builder whose first priority and level of experience is in the cause you are fighting for, who happens to have press experience as the number one weapon in their arsenal.

- **Compile an ever-evolving press list:** Keep a live spreadsheet of all your press contacts, with columns for names, emails, phone numbers, and the outlet they work for. That way you can easily copy and paste addresses into your email to press and not have to individually hunt for every contact. As you make more connections, add those names and contact information to your spreadsheet.

It's important to grow your press list and reach out to an ever-larger number of people as time progresses.

Now you may be wondering, *How do I even get reporters' emails?* You can go to a publication's website, and on the "Contact Us" page or something similar, there are usually email addresses of reporters who cover different topics. Do some internet surfing and grab those emails for your spreadsheet. You can also reach out to partner organizations and ask whether they would be willing to share a few emails or contacts. Usually, organizations are very protective of their press lists (rightfully so), so instead you can ask them to send the press release for you, if you do not have many people to send it to yourself.

- **Write out your materials:** Now it's time to write out the materials you are going to send to reporters! There are two main types of email blasts: press advisories and press releases. A press advisory is sent out days or weeks *before* an event, to alert the media what is happening and give them preliminary information: *Hey media, this will be happening soon.*

  A press release is different. It says, *Hey media, this is happening right now or has just happened!* It goes out on the day of the event, sometimes the night after the action occurs.

  Consider the scale of what you are organizing. It makes sense to send both a press advisory and release for big events. Here are examples, verbatim, of the press advisory and press release that successfully got Zero Hour coverage during our 2018 summer actions.

PRESS ADVISORY:

Media Advisory: July 10, 2018

Name of person in charge of responding to press |
email@thisisafakeemail.org

**As Heat Waves, Wildfires & Storms Shake the World,
July 21 Youth Climate March Gains Momentum**

*Sister Marches to Be Held in 25 Different Cities in US,
Europe, Africa*

Press Registration Now Open

Washington, DC—In a series of climate mobilization events
planned for later this month, Zero Hour will rally with youth
from across the world to demand immediate, commonsense
climate change legislation and draw attention to the fact that
young lives are in danger from the climate crisis.

Founded and headed by teenagers from diverse backgrounds,
Zero Hour will lead three days of events beginning July 19:
Lobby Day, Art Festival, and Youth Climate March. There
will be more than 14 sister marches in the US and across the
world, including Miami, New York City, Los Angeles, London,
São Paolo, Nuremberg, and Kenya. Many more are in the works.

Core youth organizers are available for in-person and telephonic
broadcast and print interviews. To schedule in advance, please
contact PR Person's Name,

email@thisisafakeemail.org

JULY 21—YOUTH CLIMATE MARCH

The youth will march on the National Mall to advocate for their own rights to a safe and livable future. They will rally and highlight the voices and stories of youth on the frontlines of the climate crisis.

Location	120 Constitution Ave NE, Washington, DC 20004
Time	10:30 am
Speakers	• Local Native youth and DC inter-tribal drum group will open with a song and share a few words on local indigenous resistance. • A 10-year-old DC local black activist will talk about her experiences with lack of water access. • An 18-year-old core team member will talk about how her family lost their livelihood to climate change. • An 18-year-old indigenous hip hop artist and climate activist will talk about fracking in his hometown in Colorado and sing two songs. • A coalition of youth from Standing Rock, including the founders of the whole Standing Rock movement, will speak about their experiences on the frontlines, as well as perform music and lead the crowd in chants. • Grammy-nominated actress and singer and Broadway star will sing. • The 16-year-old founder will talk about the founding of the movement and lead a die-in action to honor the lives lost in Hurricane Maria.
Press Registration	**If using an online form, insert a link**

Zero Hour, founded and led by high school students across the US, will lead the largest climate mobilization effort by youth of color in Washington, DC.

The movement has been endorsed and supported by more than 40 national and grassroots organizations, including 350.org, Sierra Club, Indigenous Environmental Network, Citizens Climate Lobby, NRDC, and others. In the past month, climate activists, scientists, and celebrities have all joined in to promote the march, including Al Gore, Chelsea Handler, Leonardo DiCaprio, Michael Mann, and Shailene Woodley.

PRESS RELEASE:

July 21st 2018
Contact: Jamie Margolin
email@thisisafakeemail.org

Shravya Jain
email@thisisafakeemail.org
333.555.6666

"We Are the Ones We've Been Waiting For":
Generation Z March for Urgent Climate Action
Sister Marches and Events in 25 Cities Around the World

Washington, DC—On Saturday, July 21, youth across the world took to the streets to draw attention to the fact that young lives are in danger from the climate crisis and demanded immediate climate action.

There were more than 25 Zero Hour sister marches and day-of-action events in the US and across the world, including gatherings in New York City, Los Angeles, Seattle, Quad Cities, London, UK, and Butere, Kenya. Collectively, this youth-led grassroots movement drew thousands.

At a rally in Washington, DC, Zero Hour organizers, the Standing Rock Youth, Havana Chapman-Edwards and DC tribal youth shared their experiences on the impacts of carbon pollution on their generation. Despite the pouring rain, the crowd cheered on Nahko and Xiuhtezcatl Martinez who sang about young people rising up, social justice and the power of protests. Then, the crowd marched from the National Mall to Lincoln Park to demand an end to business as usual on climate change.

"We are the ones we've been waiting for," said **Jamie Margolin, Zero Hour's 16-year-old founder.** "It's clear that elected leaders haven't been thinking about our future as they stall on action and continue to let fossil fuel companies pollute. Extreme weather events like this summer's heat waves and wildfires and last year's hurricanes are proof that we are already feeling the impacts of climate change. As the planet continues to warm, climate impacts will only worsen. #ThisIsZeroHour to take action."

The march capped three days mobilization activities in Washington, DC. On July 19, the Zero Hour organizers and volunteers met with nearly 50 senators and their congressional staff, including Sen. Tammy Duckworth, Sen. Bernie Sanders, Sen. Jeff Merkley, and Sen. Cortez Masto. The purpose of the Lobby Day was to educate them about Zero Hour's platform that specifies need for climate justice, including equity, racial justice, and economic justice. The youth also urged the Senators to stop accepting fossil fuel money. This was followed by an art festival on July 20th where artists and performers used art to engage the DC community for climate action and bring cultural diversity to the issue.

Zero Hour, a youth-led climate and environmental justice organization, centers the voices of diverse youth in the conversation around climate and environmental justice.

In the past month, climate activists, scientists and celebrities have publicly voiced support for the march, including Don Cheadle, Al Gore, Chelsea Handler, Leonardo DiCaprio, Michael Mann and Shailene Woodley. The movement has been endorsed and supported by more than 40 national and grassroots organizations, including 350.org, Earth Guardians, Sierra Club, Hip Hop Caucus, Indigenous Environmental Network, Citizens Climate Lobby, NRDC and others.

- **Send your materials out at strategic times:** Sending out a press release at midnight on a weekend is not your best bet if you want reporters to see your alert pop up in their inbox. Send your materials during normal business office hours on a weekday whenever possible for best response rates.

  Another important detail when you send out a press release or advisory to a large number of reporters at the same time: always bcc, never cc so that each reporter receiving the email can see the list of the hundreds of other emails that the press release or advisory is being sent to. Obviously, they can tell when an email isn't totally personalized, but there is still a psychology in actually seeing the names of hundreds of other reporters that makes them less likely to cover the story. So always bcc when sending press blasts!

- **Make personalized calls and emails to specific reporters:** From my personal conversations with reporters, the general consensus is, *Ugh, I hate press releases! They're so impersonal and make you feel like just another name on a list.* This does not mean don't send press releases; it simply means that you are going to have to do more than just send a general email blast to your list if you're heavily promoting something. Compile a shorter list of reporters to send customized emails and make calls to, and take the time to personally reach out. Reporters are more likely to respond to a carefully customized personal email than a general press release. Again—that doesn't mean don't send a press release; it means do both.

- **Take note of what is press-worthy and what isn't, and promote accordingly:** Some events, like large demonstrations, direct actions, and other flashy actions will be deemed a lot more "press-worthy" by the media than others. Don't waste your time promoting something that you don't think reporters will deem press-worthy too heavily. That doesn't mean your action is less important—it means it has a different goal. However, if there are prominent politicians, celebrities, public figures, or any sort of large, flashy, new, revolutionary event happening, make sure not only to send out press releases and advisories but to do lots of individual outreach.

WHAT TO DO WITH NEGATIVE AND INACCURATE PRESS

Sometimes the media doesn't cover things the right way. Mistakes will happen. Reporters are human, and humans mess up. Here's what you do.

- **Ignore negative press—only respond if it gets out of control:** If you get any sort of negative press, the best thing you can do is ignore it and let it blow over. As a young person in the activism space, you may experience accusations that you are a fraud and a puppet of the adults around you or a part of some big conspiracy. Take negative press as a compliment that you are making such an impact that people are starting to get intimidated. Replying to a negative news story or sharing simply amplifies that negative message. However, if there is a dangerous and false rumor that is catching on, take to your own social media channels to put out a professionally worded statement debunking the rumor. Then move on with your life.
- **Contact the press if there is factual inaccuracy:** If a publication that covered your activism or interviewed you got something important wrong, do not hesitate to reach out and fact-check. Most of the time, they will immediately correct it.
- **Create your own media:** Use social media, blogging, YouTube, and other platforms where you can shape your own narrative to correctly tell the story yourself. Upload a video to

social media and every platform you have. If you consistently upload content of your own about your activism and actions to social media, the press is likely to see it and pull from it and be more accurate in their coverage going forward.

- **Remember—you don't owe the press anything:** If there is a publication approaching you that you do not trust, is being rude or pushy, or you know is going to mess your story up, you are in no way required to give an interview. You don't owe the media anything. You are not being rude or ungrateful by politely turning an opportunity down.
- **What to do when you're doing a press interview:**
  - » **Be succinct:** In today's soundbite-driven media landscape, only small, memorable bits of conversations make the evening news and headlines. To best get your message across, you want to hit two or three points hard and stay focused on them. Do not ramble on in interviews—just say what you really want to come out in the final product, and emphasize those points throughout the interview. Stay focused. If you know an interview is coming up, it might be good to practice. What are your main talking points? What is it you most want to get across? Rehearse delivering these points until you believe you are properly getting your message across.
  - » **Only say what you would be okay seeing in print:** Press outlets revise already published articles only when there is a blatant error of fact—not if something you said in the interview was something you now regret. Reporters have every right to take your words out of context and spin them for the story however they like. So don't confide juicy gossip about yourself or your movement to a reporter who is being particularly friendly, even if you

say it's off the record. Oftentimes, those "off the record" statements make it into print. Remember, at the end of the day, a reporter's job is not to be your friend and promote your great work—it's to sell a good story.

» **Be polite and kind, but also set boundaries, and make sure those boundaries are respected:** Be confident, polite, and easygoing when you are talking with press. Act professional—but you don't have to do everything they say. If a reporter is asking you inappropriate questions you can decline to answer them. If a reporter is being too pushy and getting in your face and not respecting your time, you can end the interview. Yes, being professional and easy to work with is important, but you also need to protect yourself from the media taking advantage of your time and energy. Set your boundaries, and don't let reporters cross them. I've had documentary filmmakers want to take up every second of my time and film me in every private moment and interaction, pushing me to the max. I was drained and exhausted, and they just kept wanting more, more, *more* from me that I couldn't give. I finally just had to say, *No, I will not answer any more questions, you have enough to work with* and shut them down.

Another time, a reporter kept taking hours of my time and the time of my Zero Hour team on the phone answering endless questions for weeks. The day before the article came out, the reporter tried calling my team and me *again*. We were patient and gave so much time and energy, and they kept draining and draining us. Eventually we just said, "You have what you need," and didn't take any more phone calls with them. We set boundaries and reminded ourselves that we didn't owe the media anything. If we felt like we had given them all the information they needed, then that was that. The actual article that resulted didn't even include much of what we talked about—it was all information that could have been easily pulled from other articles about Zero Hour.

WHEN YOU DON'T GET PRESS . . .

Sometimes the press just decides not to cover you. They don't show up to your events, and they don't highlight your voice or your movement. I can't count the amount of well-crafted press releases I've sent to reporters with not a single news article coming out of it. Sometimes the thing you are pitching does not fit the news cycle or pique the interest of reporters at the time. And that's okay. It happens. A lot. I'd say about 99.9 percent of the work I do goes uncovered by press. The vast majority of what we as organizers and activists do is behind-the-scenes grunt work, and that's okay.

As you work hard applying press strategies to get your activism covered in the media, always keep in the forefront of your mind that your worth as an activist is not dictated by the amount of press you get. Worldwide fame for being a youth activist is rare, fleeting, and often accidental. You can never predict what action, campaign, or movement is going to happen at the right place at the right time with the right person who will make the whole thing blow up. Sometimes actions and campaigns that completely change the world happen quietly, with hardly any media coverage. Revolutionary grassroots change is happening in communities all over the world thanks to activists whose names the world doesn't know. If you are one of those organizers who has been working tirelessly behind the scenes, transforming your community and doing the work that needs to be done regardless of whether the cameras are on or not—thank you. You are a rock star, and it doesn't matter if not a single article has been written about you and your work. Organizers like you make the world go 'round and are the backbone of every movement.

Falling into the hole of *but I started before that person and they're getting more attention* is not healthy, because there is always someone who came before you. People can rise to fame in the blink of an eye, and others will work for years, even decades, with little to no glory. It's just the reality of the job and the way media operates. That's why you have to stay grounded in your *why,* because your *why* will keep you motivated and ready to keep fighting even when the credit and cameras do not come. The press often covers the person who lit the fire, not the people who spend years laying the kindling so the fire will catch and spread.

The bottom line is, employing the right tactics, we as youth have the power to shape the media and, by default, the hearts and minds of millions of people. With media attention, one small action can spread into a worldwide movement that changes everything. Because we as youth do not have a voice in government or in judicial and financial sectors, the free press is a valuable tool to get our causes and stories out into the world and change lives.

Freedom of the press is not something to take for granted if you are from a country that has it. It is amazing and game changing for a movement to take over the press—as long as you make sure the press doesn't take over *you.*

Andrea Alejandra Gonzales, Eighteen, She/Her
Youth Over Guns community organizer for gender equality, racial justice, decolonization, and gun violence prevention

JAMIE: How did you become an activist?

ANDREA: My school took down a photography project I did about abolishing rape culture, photos of women posing nude with different words painted on their backs like "No means No." The school took it down, claiming it was "pornographic."

I made forms and an online petition to put my artwork back. The students generated enough outrage that I got interviewed by news outlets. My photos ended up in the Metropolitan Museum of Art.

Two weeks after the Parkland school shooting, there was a threat in my school. My school was in lockdown for about three hours, without service. There was no clear information.

When the police arrived, they had gigantic guns and were aggressive and hostile. They didn't help the situation.

JAMIE: How does being an indigenous, Latina, queer woman affect your activism?

ANDREA: Being indigenous and carrying the trauma of my parents and ancestors is hard. I've been in a lot of activist spaces where people try to explain my own trauma to me.

I use "queer" as an umbrella term. I am fluid with my sexuality and tend to fall on the feminine side, so people assume I'm straight. But it is still a big part of who I am, what I fight for. The effects of homophobia are real.

JAMIE: **What are your strategies for creating change?**

ANDREA: I demand a revolution. I see liberation as being ready to die for something.

My goal is fighting for the end of all violence. Violence is not having water and food, or being systematically pushed into the prison system. I work toward that goal by educating people through workshops and events and talking to people who are marginalized, and on giving communities the language and vocabulary they need to empower themselves.

JAMIE: **What are your tips for young women of color activists?**

ANDREA: All your unique experiences lead up to this moment, and no one else can lead the way you can. I lead through a lot of love and tenderness. We are our ancestors' wildest dreams. We are here for a reason.

JAMIE: **Thoughts on the media's influence on the contemporary culture of youth activism?**

ANDREA: It's so amazing to see this big, visible wave of young people. But lately I have been noticing there are a lot of youth who do "activism" for a college recommendation, then abandon the community the minute they get what they need.

11

MAKING YOUR ACTIVISM GO VIRAL

USING SOCIAL MEDIA AS A WEAPON TO CREATE MASSIVE CHANGE.

Used correctly, social media can be a weapon wielded to create massive change. Social media can start movements, connect you to like-minded activists all around the world, and offer a significant tool for organizing. Used incorrectly, social media can turn you into a "clicktivist" and make you lose sight of why you're doing the work you do, make you hungry for clout, instant gratification, and the appearance of being an #Activist without actually making concrete change in your community.

If it weren't for social media, I would have never been able to start the international youth climate justice movement Zero Hour. Zero Hour began with an Instagram post. Nadia Nazar, who had read an op-ed I wrote about climate change in Teen Ink, saw it and messaged me that she wanted to help make this movement a reality, even though she lived on the opposite side of the United States.

A few more people reached out—also from vastly different parts of the country. I started messaging climate justice activists I followed online about the Youth Climate March, and gradually we built a team of diverse youth that spanned from Seattle to the Standing Rock Reservation, to Baltimore, to North Carolina, to Atlanta, to Los Angeles.

Back in 2017 the youth climate movement had not yet become mainstream—this was before the #FridaysForFuture climate strikes, before the Extinction Rebellion, before the Green New Deal grew in popularity, before it was popular to be a young climate justice activist. So for an entire year, we had to build momentum for the Youth Climate March that would take place in July 2018. We kept building and raising awareness, connecting with other organizations on social media, and advertising our actions online. We connected with influencers and social justice activists on Twitter and Instagram and shared the Facebook event for the Youth Climate March far and wide.

Social media connected us and allowed us to create Zero Hour. It helped us grow. We used it to spread the word about the Youth Climate March and connect with media outlets to cover it. Through social media we connected with organizers all over the world, who organized sister marches in their communities. Social media allowed us to broadcast images and videos from the Youth Climate Marches all over the world, which were noticed and amplified by prominent politicians, celebrities, organizations, and influencers voicing their public support for the movement. Thousands of young people all around the world were inspired to take climate action from our actions. Through social media, we now maintain contact with our global community of climate justice activists and continue to amplify climate action events and educate about climate justice.

To be clear, social media was just one part of a complex movement-building strategy that took a whole team and lots of hard work to execute. Zero Hour is not entirely social media work—the vast majority of it is phone and conference calls, email chains, community educational events, public speaking, summits, lobby days, and mobilizations. We do real community organizing work, and social media is simply one tactic to build and grow the movement and to communicate with people around the world.

Social media used in the right way can change your life and change the world. Are you ready to use the accounts at your fingertips to make change? Here is what you need to know.

SOCIAL MEDIA ACTIVISM 101: CURATING A SOCIAL MEDIA STRATEGY FOR A CAMPAIGN, EVENT, OR ORGANIZATION

- **Decide on your core messaging and talking points:** What are you broadcasting? Is it an event you're putting on? An organization you're launching? A campaign you're starting? Whatever it is, come up with a relatively short but catchy name for it, and craft the core messages you want people to understand. These key pieces of information need to fit into a tweet or a short Facebook or Instagram post. What you want to do is convey what you are organizing, why it is important, and what are the main pieces of information that people need to know. For example:

NAME: THE YOUTH CLIMATE MARCH

Main talking points:

  » This is Zero Hour to act on climate change.
  » The youth have had enough of our leaders putting polluters over our lives, so we are marching to demand a livable future.

» We need to get down to 350 parts per million of carbon in the atmosphere by the end of the twenty-first century for civilization on earth to continue.

Information:

» Youth are organizing marches all over the world for climate justice. Everyone who believes in the cause is welcome to attend.

» Visit thisiszerohour.org for dates, times, and details of attending the marches.

- **Decide on hashtags and a tag:** Hashtags and a tag (the actual account where people can find all the information they need) are crucial if you want the word to spread far and wide. You need unified messaging, keywords, and phrases people can search to find your cause. Hashtags—something short and catchy that links social media posts under one cohesive campaign—are vital. Come up with two or three main hashtags for your campaign that are short, memorable, descriptive, and fairly unique to you.

  Let's say you are launching an empowerment campaign for teenage girls, and you want the hashtag to be "#GirlPower"— that would not be a smart move. That hashtag is so widely used that your project would get lost in it all. The hashtag you come up with for your campaign needs to be unique and original, something that will immediately make people think of what you're organizing, not something that could describe a hundred different things. So for that teenage girl empowerment campaign, instead try a hashtag like #GenZGirlGang (an actual initiative you should check out, by the way).

  TAG: @THISISZEROHOUR

  Hashtags: #ThisIsZeroHour, #YouthClimateMarch, #ClimateJusticeNow

- **Create graphics, visuals, and cohesive branding—and spread it:** You need to have visuals to go along with what you are talking about—have a set of colors, fonts, and a certain design that people can start to associate with what you are doing. This is not applicable to every action and campaign, but it is for most. Look for someone with experience in graphic design to help you come up with the best cohesive branding. Consistent branding is important to build a recognizable movement. Let's think about your favorite company. If all of their stores and advertising had different logos, fonts, and color spectrums, just an overall different branding, it would be super confusing and hard to unify all of those stores and ads under the one umbrella of that company. The same goes for your activism!

- **Time your posts—make a post calendar and post consistently (but don't spam!):** For anything to catch on, you have to post consistently. You cannot just throw one or two posts out there and expect the word to spread. A good social media strategy means planned and consistent content going out to build a narrative. Don't spam and post nonstop because that is also counterproductive, but I would say posting three or four times a week at least is a good idea when you are spreading the word about a new organization, event, or campaign. Create a social media calendar where you plan out the programing for your initiative's social media channels. You can have specific campaigns for different weekdays, like #FunFactFriday or #TipTuesday or #LivestreamMonday, as well as special content for holidays (like Earth Day, Women's Day, etc.). I would advise consulting with people who have worked on a social media strategy for a campaign similar to yours beforehand and making sure you have a balanced and consistent flow of content.

- **Have an ask in your posts, and make it accessible:** Your social media posts about your campaign should have an ask for those who see it to take action. Something like, "donate," "RSVP," "share with your friends," and then a link for them to take that action. You want your ask to be accessible on that post and easily done by anyone scrolling through their phones. People have busy lives and will not go hunting around the internet for the materials you talk about, even if they have some interest in your cause. The link should be placed directly in the post or directly explained. Your goal is not just to have as many people as possible see the message but for them to take meaningful action off it.

Action Items:

» Sign up HERE (then you would insert a link to the information) to attend a march near you!

» Donate HERE to help us fund our actions!

» Tag a friend below to let them know about this event!

» Click HERE to sign up to volunteer!

- **Make a social media tool kit and share it widely:** When you first throw something out into the internet void, it's very rare that it catches on and spreads like wildfire after one post. You need to create materials for members of other organizations, your friends, influencers you reach out to, and any other allies to share and amplify what you're doing. This is a social media tool kit. Curate sample posts that you want others to post on their social media channels—these curated posts should include tags, hashtags, and any graphics and photos you want posted. Your tool kit should include curated post options for every social media outlet, as well as any guidelines that you want those posting to follow.

Once you complete the tool kit, email it to everyone you know who would be willing to post about the project you're working on. Having others post their endorsement will start to make your cause appear more often on people's feeds. The more people post about that cohesive message, the more your movement will grow.

THINGS TO BE WARY OF WHEN USING SOCIAL MEDIA AS A TOOL TO MAKE CHANGE

- **Being a clicktivist:** Clicktivism is when the extent of your activism is simply retweeting and posting your opinions on social media and maybe the occasional picture of yourself with a sign at a march or rally. A clicktivist doesn't actually use social media as one of the many tools in their toolbox to make real change; social media is the end-all of their activism.

  You have to remember that although social media holds power to influence, there is a limit to its reach. A social media post might pressure someone to take action or raise awareness on a topic, but tweeting by itself does not stop a pipeline, change a law, or aid your community. In the end you are just throwing 1s and 0s out into the internet void if you are not actually taking the bulk of your work offline with the real people, animals, places, and communities you want to help. Simply telling those who follow you on the internet "I'm woke and care about this cause!" does not necessarily help the cause.

  Social media should be a tool to amplify the real work that is happening, in real life. If all social media platforms were to disappear from the face of the earth this instant, you should still have a large part of your activism intact. If the end of social media would be the end of your activism—that's not a good sign. If the extent of your activism is posting opinions online, it's time to accept you've fallen into the clicktivist trap and get out there and do some real community organizing!

- **Clout chasing and curating the trendy appearance of being an #Activist:** Social media makes it easy for us put on a façade.

It's important to not get hooked on the numbers, such as how many followers, likes, shares, and retweets you get. What can start to happen is you become addicted to this constant approval and veneration from others, so your activism begins to turn superficial, rather than actually moving the needle toward change. Have you noticed you go to a protest simply for the good Instagram visual of you holding a sign? Do you tend to be more preoccupied with getting all of the right pictures of an action so you can have the best-curated social media content, rather than with how the action is going in real life and whether it is effective? Do you find yourself losing interest in tasks that don't make for anything social media–worthy? Are you constantly thinking about the numbers you are getting on social media, how many followers you have, and how many people have complimented you on your last "#Activist" post? Are you losing track of your *why* and the actual end goal of your cause, instead are you more focused on getting acclaim, awards, and gaining social media popularity? Are you doing things because they would get you more clout online, even if they don't actually make strategic sense in advancing the cause you're fighting for?

If any of these assessments are true (and I am not saying this to make you feel guilty—we're all still learning and growing), I would advise you to temporarily delete the social media apps from your phone for a little bit and take some time to recenter. Get rid of that constant validation from social media for a little while, and reflect on your *why* and what got you fighting for this cause in the first place.

- **Falling for the hate:** Yes, by all means use your social platforms to engage people and get feedback—but do not let hateful comments on social media define your opinions of yourself or the work you do. If people online are threatening you, making you feel terrible about the work you do, invalidating you, hating on you, calling you names, or coming after different aspects of your identity, don't let it get to you.

The only time you should react and give any of your emotional energy to a hate comment is if it could be a threat to your safety. In that case, screenshot the message for evidence, report the harasser, and immediately talk to a trusted adult about it. You have things to do, places to be, movements to run, people who love you, and time is precious—don't waste it letting what some creep online said about you or your work get to you.

- **Trash talking others, posting inappropriate things about yourself:** As an activist it is important that you stay professional online. This means no lashing out at your allies on the internet, no profane content, no inappropriate content about your friends or yourself; even if it seems like a joke, it often isn't interpreted that way. Those who oppose you are already looking to undermine you anyway—don't give them free material to do so.

Now, what counts as "inappropriate"? Well, any videos and photos of you partying, for example, should not be put online. Even if you post it on a private account, nothing online is totally private, and even if you delete something, what goes on the internet never really goes away. Maybe photos and videos of you acting up at a party are cool to personally show your friends, but never publicly post something online that you would not be okay with your senator seeing. That might sound silly, but it's generally a good guideline. Envision a politician scrolling through your feed. Things can be taken out of context so easily, even if they're totally aboveboard. Another way to think about it is to post only what you would be okay with a college admissions officer seeing.

What not to post about your fellow activists and people in the movement: don't post about other activists what you would not want posted about you. If you have an issue with someone else in the movement, take it up directly with them. No public callouts, please!

So yes, social media is a great tool, but like any tool, it's important to be careful and not use it in a harmful way!

Now, just because this marks the end of this chapter does not mean that this is the end-all, be-all of social media strategy. Social media can help you not only with campaigns and event organizing but also with raising awareness and sharing about your own personal life and experiences. Continually telling your story and pushing a narrative that society doesn't usually accept is a form of activism in itself. "The Unapologetically Brown Series" is a perfect example of how social media can be used to amplify a movement, or be a movement and community within itself. Founded by Johanna Toruño, the visual series utilizes public space for storytelling by queer People of Color. The hugely popular Instagram account highlights Johanna's street art and serves as an online community where queer People of Color can see themselves represented. The content she shares on Instagram serves as a form of activism.

With social media, you have the incredible ability to connect with people from all over the world and spread a message farther and more quickly than ever before. Uncensored social media access is a privilege of free countries, as many authoritarian states ban or censor use of international social media apps. Why? Because knowledge is power, and so is communication, and authoritarian states fear the power of the people when they have access to external knowledge and the ability to transcend the narratives they are indoctrinated into in their countries. So do not take that power for granted, and do not waste it on chasing external approval and instant gratification. Use it strategically to organize movements and spread your message. The world is at your fingertips.

Ezra Greyson Wheeler, Twenty, They/Them
Founder of the We Exist Collective
and Just a Bunch of Kids

JAMIE: How would you describe yourself?

EZRA: I am a twenty-year-old accomplished activist, speaker, and writer. I also happen to be chronically ill. I have Ehlers-Danlos syndrome, which is a disorder that affects my connective tissues supporting my skin, bones, blood vessels, and many other vital organs and tissues.

I am the founder of We Exist, a social movement to include disabled people in activism and start a real conversation about ableism. I am passionate about disability rights, including health-care legislation, as well as women's rights and queer rights.

JAMIE: What are your artistic mediums and what drew you to those mediums?

EZRA: A lot of it is digital art that is used for activism to be amplified on social media. I make a lot of things that can go on a sticker and a button, and I've designed and drawn social media posts that talk about the issues of disability and queerness and start a conversation. I was drawn to doing digital art on my iPad due to the fact that I couldn't draw for a long time because my wrists got bad due to my Ehlers-Danlos syndrome, so that was a more accessible way of making art.

JAMIE: **How does your queerness affect your artwork?**

EZRA: My queerness affects my poetry because I write a lot about queer love. I write from experience and draw and take photos from experience. People often ask me, "Why does *everything* have to be about being LGBTQ+?" And it's because I am! I write, draw, paint, from my experience.

JAMIE: **What does accessibility for people with disabilities look like?**

EZRA: Accessibility is so much more than having wheelchair ramps. It is this all-encompassing idea that disabled people don't have special needs, we have different needs. It's about wheelchair-accessible spaces and accessible parking—but it's also always having a sign language interpreter at events, printing things in Braille. The part that is overlooked is making sure that the environment is safe and inviting for disabled people. That looks like having disabled people in the planning and execution stages of the event. Having dedicated resources.

12

ACTIVISM AND YOUR CRAZY LIFE

SNEAKING A FEW CONFERENCE CALLS IN THE BATHROOM DURING LUNCH . . .

My junior year of high school, when I was interviewing with my editor to clinch the deal for this very book you are reading, it was lunchtime, and I was hiding from my friends in my school's costume closet. I was pacing around the tiny room in the back of my school's theater department, passionately making the case for why my generation needs this book to help us drive change in the movement.

I had to cut the call short because my friends were standing outside the door. The bell had just rung, and if I didn't hang up at that moment, I would be late for class.

I spent the entirety of algebra not paying attention and panicking that I had totally screwed up that interview. But you're reading this so . . . it worked out okay.

Being a busy young person with a whole life outside of your activism is a juggling act. It means not just finding time but *making* time for your work.

There is (usually) no such thing as "not having" time. We all, when you boil it down, *have* time. Whether we prioritize it and what we put that time to is up to us.

This chapter is all about how to prioritize, balance, juggle, and make time in your life to be a successful young activist—whatever that means to you.

Let's be clear, being a successful youth activist does not look like only one thing. "Successful" doesn't mean fame, it doesn't have to mean starting some massive organization, it doesn't mean writing a book (see what I did there?)—it means whatever it is that you want it to be, whatever holds up your *why.*

Before we get into strategies for managing your time so you can make the most difference possible within your schedule, I need you to get the corporate idea of success out of your mind. Success as a changemaker is not like success on the corporate ladder. Unlike success in sports, school, or jobs, activist success is not about doing "better" than other people or being "the best" at something. It's not an activist competition to get the most accolades, awards, achievements, followers, or just "make the biggest change" in general.

This is not about pure self-advancement, and success is not equal to clout. This is best explained by young environmental activist Sophia Manolis, in her 2019 op-ed for the *South High Southerner:*

This desire to be noticed is natural and human, but at the same time I believe it can be distracting and destructive. Although I do not want to hide my voice (I am using it now after all) or my passion, I realize that disproportionate attention focused on me or any single individual who lands in the spotlight can shadow other activists in this movement, especially those who have worked longer and harder without much attention. Why should my work be put on a higher pedestal than theirs? Is there really anything that makes me more special?

The truth is that "activism" can and must be practiced in many ways that often go unnoticed. It is listening and building relationships. It's writers who focus on issues and perspectives outside the status quo. It's teachers who lift up marginalized voices and try to also learn from their students. It's prison inmates reading books to educate themselves about politics and business. It is being what society deems "other" or "not normal" and yet radically loving yourself. As people focus on "trendy" activism—youth who get attention from the media, give powerful speeches at rallies, and attempt to do the biggest and flashiest possible things—we (myself very much included) have to remember that those attention-generating strategies are not the only way to create change. As activists, we must keep educating ourselves, listening to other perspectives, and remembering to be aware as much as possible. We must challenge ourselves not to just advocate for "our own" issues, but strive to lift up other issues, voices who aren't being heard, and ways in which issues intersect. We must be humble, and we must be okay with discomfort. We must follow our morals instead of following attention and/or perceived "success."

At the same time, we are all on a journey to find our own strengths and passions and use them for good, to make this type of daily "activism" a norm in every occupation and community. That work is often hard, it's not flashy, it can go against the societal expectation of being complacent and following rules, but it's so important. Whoever you are, you can be an activist too—you just have to figure out the way that will work best for you.

I'm going to be honest with you—being a student and an activist at the same time can be hectic! Sometimes it means taking conference calls during lunch, replying to emails during home-room, calling congressional policy assistants on the bus ride home, and posting on social media about your upcoming actions when the teacher isn't looking (don't do that, please pay atten-tion in class). It can sometimes mean sacrificing downtime, social activities, time with family, and often sleep. It sometimes means sacrificing other things that you really want for the movement you are a part of. You get to decide what stays and what goes and how you balance your time.

If you're reading this and are panicking that being an activist means you need to give up everything good and fun in your life, chill. You get to decide how much you want to sacrifice and how much of your life you want to devote to a cause.

And if you're like me and your life's work is your activism, you still need to learn how to balance your life. No protest or project or movement is worth wrecking a relationship with close friends or family, or missing an important life experience or spe-cial occasion. You hear me? None.

I learned this the hard way. I am a workaholic who spends way more time in my inbox than with my parents and friends. I am the kind of overly productive and ambitious girl who sets her brain on autopilot, shuts off her emotions, and sometimes tunes out of what matters most in life. It's made me depressed, anxious, grumpy, and tired a lot. My activism has put a strain on my rela-tionships with my friends; they are often very upset that I seem to have more time for conference calls than them. One time my little cousin told my mom, "I'm sad because Jamie chose her work over her family," and it broke my heart. It's not healthy.

Please do not sacrifice your health for a movement. As some-one who has done it time and time again, it's just not worth it, and it doesn't even help in the long run. Why? Because sacrificing the things that make you happy for your cause makes you resent your cause more and more, and this leads to burnout. If you are burned out, you will not put in the same amount of energy and love into the cause as you could, and you will end up with lower-quality actions, events, and results.

These are my tips to live by, how to juggle your activism when you have school, homework, parents and family, and extracurriculars you need to balance as well!

HOW TO FIT YOUR ACTIVISM INTO YOUR CRAZY-BUSY LIFE

- **Change the way you think about time. It's not about having time, it's about *making* time:** You have time to be a change-maker and fight for a cause. Period. I don't know you, I don't know your schedule, but I know you have time. There are 168 hours in a week. If you go to school or work a full-time job, roughly 40 hours a week, and are sleeping 8 hours a night, so 56 hours a week—that leaves 72 hours a week for your activism. Let's say you also spend 10 hours a week doing a sport, an extracurricular, or fulfilling some sort of family responsibility. That still leaves 62 hours for your activism. Let's say you also want to have a social life and downtime—you want to spend 10 hours a week hanging out with friends and family and just living life and watching TV. That still leaves 52 hours for your activism. Fifty-two hours is a lot of time to make a big difference.

    If you make activism a serious priority in your life, you will start to see that there really is time.

    Sometimes you literally don't have time for something, and that's totally okay ... but often "I don't have time" really means "it's not a priority."

- **Use every spare second you get:** Have a long bus ride home from school? Instead of aimlessly scrolling through Instagram and comparing your life to others, make those calls that you need to make. Got to class five minutes early? Take the time to make a social media post about that fundraising event you have coming up. You're watching a show and there are previews? Open your laptop and send a few emails.

  You get the picture.... our lives are full of pockets of five, ten minutes that can each be used to advance your cause. We often discard these little moments, but they really add up. Using each and every spare minute you have wisely can really help you get ahead.

- **Find a school/activism balance:** What's the secret to balancing being a student and an activist? DON'T MULTITASK. It doesn't make you more productive or get you ahead; it just makes your brain hurt and makes you half-ass both things you were supposed to be working on.

  If you are in class at school, don't ignore what's going on and send emails instead. Be present in the classroom, pay attention, and take good notes. I am telling you this because I am someone who has spent pretty much my entire high school career not paying attention in class trying to multitask and do my activism work at school. I thought I was being an extra-savvy youth activist nailing my school/activism balance by doing my activist work in class. But it didn't work out—at all. Bad, bad idea.

  What ends up happening is that over time you stop understanding the subject matter of your classes, so you end up spending way more time studying at home and after school, and your grades drop. Once your grades drop and you do badly on tests, that's more added homework, test corrections, and studying you have to do. All that extra time studying at home could have been used to work on your activism if you had just been present at school. Being present at school and paying close attention also will save you so much stress and fighting with your parents about grades.

When you're at school, you're at school. It's okay to set healthy boundaries for yourself. When you're in history class, you're in history class—not texting members of your organization under the desk, writing emails, or planning—you're in class. When you're on a call, you're not scrolling through Instagram or checking your emails at the same time—you're on that call.

Whatever you are doing, be fully present. Do only one thing at a time. That is way more strategic and productive than trying to do fifty things at once. Do tasks well, and then you don't have to do them again or do damage control.

Answer texts and emails, work on that grant proposal, whatever it is you need to do, in between classes and during breaks, never during class!

- **Keep daily to-do lists:** If you are already a person who keeps a detailed to-do list or planner, keep it up! For those of you who are not in the habit of making daily to-do lists that you check and work off, now is time to start. The best way to manage everything on your plate (or everything that should be on your plate) is to write it all down. Keep a Google calendar, a notes app on your phone, or an old fashioned notebook with your tasks for each day. If you weren't able to complete the task you were supposed to today, transfer it to tomorrow's list. I like using a planner so I can lay out my tasks for the week and think ahead.

  Lists help you remember everything you're supposed to do, stay on track, and declutter your brain. Use them!

- **Make a list of what you are and are not willing to sacrifice for your activism, and take action accordingly:** Keep in mind, sleeping, eating, and basic self-sustenance should not be on your list—that is not on the table to cut. Sorry, it's just not an option. You have to take care of yourself.

Here is an example of the list I made of big time-consuming tasks in my life plus activities I want to potentially devote my time to in the near future.

JAMIE'S LIST OF STUFF IN HER LIFE

- » School + homework
- » Hanging out with my friends
- » Spending time with a girl I'm dating (if I occasionally happen to not be single)
- » Watching Netflix/TV
- » Spending time with family
- » Listening to music
- » Being on social media
- » College essay work
- » College applications
- » Drivers ed
- » SAT studying
- » Attending concerts, dances, parties, and other fun social events
- » Working on local climate justice efforts in Seattle
- » Doing speaking engagements and attending/participating in climate justice and youth events outside of my own organization
- » Doing the daily grunt work for my organization and planning our mass climate justice actions
- » Writing op-eds and my book

On this list, a few items stood out to me right away that I can NOT cut out. School and homework, for obvious reasons. Others are a bit more personal to me—I am a writer and it's vital for me to carve out time to write, so that also can't be cut. But I cut drivers ed temporarily because where and the way I live, I don't need to devote time to it right this minute. I also cut attending school dances and social events, and some social media time because those are all things that are less important to me, and I'm willing to give them up in order to have more time to fight for climate justice (I will attend a concert or a dance once or twice a year). Netflix and listening to music are crucial self-care practices for me that I cannot cut out, but I can certainly spend less time on them when needed.

Sometimes I use one-woman dance parties in my room or Netflix as unhealthy ways of avoiding my own feelings and responsibilities, so that self-sabotage can definitely be cut from my schedule. When I was studying for the SAT, I shrank (at least attempted to) my Netflix/music time to fit that in. As for spending time with friends, family, or a girl I'm into, I am willing to sacrifice some of it but obviously not all of it. Maintaining human relationships and not becoming a total socially isolated hermit is a priority to me, but I do tend to lean toward prioritizing my activism over my personal relationships. I had the opportunity to visit my family in Colombia in the summer of 2018, but it was at the same time as the 2018 Youth Climate March, so I chose to protest in the pouring rain in Washington, DC, instead of taking a vacation in my family's home country and being fed delicious Colombian food by people who love me. We all have to make sacrifices for our work sometimes.

What does *your* list look like? What in your life are you willing to cut out or cut back on to make more time to pursue your cause? What in your life is vital to your happiness and well-being that you can't cut out?

- **Explain to your teachers, employers, friends, and family what you are doing and why (if that is a safe option for you):**

My activism has led me to miss tons of school, so it is super important for me to have good communication with the attendance office, my teachers, and the school administration in general. When it comes to balancing school and extracurriculars with your activism, one of the most helpful things you can do is get everyone on the same page as much as you can. It is always better for those around you to know what you are doing and what you need from them to stay on track with everything with school, your job, and so on. Have open and honest conversations with your teachers, counselors, family members, employers, and friends about what you're working on. Explain to them what this will mean for your schedule and what you will do on your end to make up for everything you miss.

It is important for teachers and employers to know that you are willing to go the distance to reach out, communicate, do the extra credit and makeup work, and just stay on top of your game.

- **Making time and working when your parents are abusive/neglectful/unsupportive of your activism:** The sad reality is that often young people's parents are not supportive of the activism work their kids do. Maybe you live in an ideologically divided household where what you're fighting for is the exact opposite of what your parents believe in. Maybe you are not mentally, emotionally, or physically safe at home. I have too many activist friends who share similar stories of abusive parents or parents who go out of their way to stop them from pursuing their activism. The best thing you can do to manage your time as an activist in a scenario like that is to be gentle with yourself and make sure you are putting your safety first. Find pockets of time when you can squeeze in calls, emails, or whatever your work entails that won't interfere with your homelife. Never feel guilty if you can't get something done or can't go to an event because you have to prioritize your safety. In an unstable, unsafe household, your self-preservation comes first. Always. Just because you get less work done for the cause does not mean you are any less worthy or any less of an activist than another young person who lives in a safe, supportive household and gets more done. Your worth as a changemaker and a person is not defined by the amount of progress you produce. As long as you are trying your best with what you have, fitting in work when you can, when it's safe for the circumstance you're in, that is enough.

I cannot emphasize enough how much your safety and well-being come first. How are you going to do a good job movement building if you aren't even doing okay yourself? Do as much as you can and, whatever you have to do to survive your bad living situation, get out of there as fast as you can. Manage your time the best you can, and if you don't get everything done that you wanted to, that's okay. Once you're out of that toxic space and have control over your own schedule, then you can follow the tips above about being the most productive activist you can be.

Be kind, gentle, and patient with yourself and remember, as iconic activist Audre Lorde once said, self-preservation "is an act of political warfare."

No matter what level of privilege you have, you can create habits, rituals, and practices to optimize your time and be the most successful young activist you can.

When it comes down to it, though these tips and tricks can be helpful, there is no one magic trick to get everything you need done and to manage your time. It all comes down to just, well, doing it—making the time to do the activism close to your heart, whether you technically "have time" or not.

Keep daily to-do lists (and stick to them), map out your commitments, decide what in your life stays and what goes, and make the most out of every single day!

Navraj Singh, Seventeen, He/Him
Activist for youth inclusion in politics and advocacy, works with Mobilizing Youth Project and Women's March Youth Empower

JAMIE: **How did you become an activist?**

NAVRAJ: After the midterms of 2018, I saw so many young people getting into politics and becoming the forefront of movements. Before that, I thought I was too young to make a difference. My first experience was at the school level—walkout for gun violence prevention. I also organized a Town Hall for Our Lives in Virginia. My friends and I kept the traction going. We started an organization called the Mobilizing Youth Project, which gave young people networks and resources to start their activism. We organize around different issues and help youth engage civically. We do internship recruitment to have youth have their voices in campaigns. I was one of the organizers of the 2019 National Youth Climate Strike in DC and Virginia. A friend of mine asked if I wanted to help. I didn't have experience in climate activism, but I jumped in!

JAMIE: **What guides you in your activism?**

NAVRAJ: Being a Sikh American. My family's faith has values that root me in what I am fighting for. Some of the main values include advocating for those who can't, the poor, the disadvantaged. Being brave enough to be a warrior and light in the darkness. *Seva*, selfless service, is the value I most live by. If I see a problem in the world, I need to speak out and try to make change.

JAMIE: **What is your strategy for creating change?**

NAVRAJ: Start at the community level, where you can make the most impact. The place you know the best, understand issues and the people.

JAMIE: **How do you balance being an activist and a student?**

NAVRAJ: Student/activist balance? Please give me the number of someone who has figured it out! Education is a privilege not to take for granted. But do you need an A+ or solutions to gun violence and climate change? You should never feel guilty for prioritizing school over your work. Our world still requires us to do school. If you have to take a week off from your activism to catch up, that's fine!

JAMIE: **What are your tips for youth with immigrant parents?**

NAVRAJ: I am a first-generation American. At first, my mom wouldn't let me do clubs or extracurriculars, let alone organize. I started doing smaller things outside of school and kept my grades up. I showed my mom that I could follow my passion and keep my grades up.

A DAY IN THE LIFE OF
A TEEN ACTIVIST

THE HOURLY BREAKDOWN OF A DAY
IN A TEEN ACTIVIST'S LIFE.

All those tips about time management are great and all, you might be thinking, *but what does life as a young activist on a day-by-day basis look like?*

To answer your question and help give you some ideas of how to start forming your own schedules and routines, here is a walk-through of my typical school weekday schedule. I hope this helps you come up with ideas of how to squeeze your activism into your school schedule.

DISCLAIMER: This is just me honestly telling you what my life as a young activist in high school is, in the day-to-day grunt work. It is NOT a model, guide, or template of what an activist's ideal day should look like; it is just what *my* day looks like. Everyone has different lives, living situations, and circumstances to work around, and I admit I lead a pretty comfortable, privileged life at the moment of writing this. So don't feel pressured to model your life after this; just take what you can out of my schedule as one example of what the day-to-day could look like as a teen organizer.

A TYPICAL HIGH SCHOOL DAY IN JAMIE'S LIFE

5:30 a.m.: Rise and shine! It's still dark outside, but if it's a weekday I have to be out of bed to get ready for school.

6:30 a.m.: After stomaching whatever I can eat this early, it's time to get in the carpool. I post on social media for Zero Hour's accounts and my personal accounts, respond to direct messages, emails, texts. The workday begins bright and early for me.

7:00 a.m.: I arrive at school an hour early, which means I have an hour to finish the homework I didn't get to the night before and cram for all the tests and quizzes I didn't study for because I was on conference calls or sorting through the hellhole that is my email.

8:00 a.m.–9:45 a.m.: Time for class! These are the first two classes of the day, and I do my best to stay awake. Hopefully by this time I've finished all my homework right before it's due (but probably not).

9:45 a.m.–10:00 a.m.: Break time! In my high school we get fifteen minutes of break after our first two classes, so I head to the locker room and hang out with my friends.

10:00 a.m.–11:45 a.m.: This is a repeat of the first two periods of the day. In between walking up the steps to my next classes, trying to listen to music, I get notifications like this from people in my organization:

> Hey Jamie, check your email I think there may be a big problem.
>
> Can you look over the grant proposal before I send it?
>
> Call me, our debit card isn't letting us book the venue.

BIG PROBLEM, I think we might have upset a
congress member, we need to do damage control
on this ASAP.

Did you make the agenda for today's call yet?

I try to focus in class, but my head will usually be spinning
from these messages and thinking ahead to when I can find the
spare minutes here and there to address everything being thrown
at me. But I find a way to put everything away and try to comprehend math before going back to the never-ending demands of
running a nonprofit.

11:50 a.m.–12:00 p.m.: Homeroom time! I will use these ten minutes either to cram for an upcoming test, finish homework I
still haven't done for my next classes, chat with my friends, or
post on social media for my personal account or my organization's account.

12:00 p.m.–12:40 p.m.: Lunchtime! I used to take calls during
lunch, but lately I've been practicing self-care and setting
boundaries for myself. It's crucial to my self-preservation
as an activist that I spend time with my friends every day at
lunch, talking about something other than activism.

On Fridays, I practice a different type of activism that I usually
don't get to do too much of—restorative community healing. I
participate in a support group for queer kids, and we all gather in
a classroom together where we can be ourselves. We vent about
homophobic and transphobic family members, we support each
other in our coming-out processes, and we simply have fun and
joke around, being in community with each other.

The support group is a form of activism in itself—a space to be resilient, connect, bond, and heal with fellow members of the LGBTQ+ community. Remember: being with and caring for your community can be a form of activism in itself that is just as important as staging a protest.

12:45 p.m.–2:30 p.m.: Last two periods of the day! I ignore the texts and emails coming in about things I need to be doing for the climate movement and just buckle down and get through with the school day. The bell finally rings at 2:30, and I pack my bags, chat with my friends, and then get my butt out of that building.

2:30 p.m.–4:00 p.m.: Usually around this time is when Zero Hour has our important calls: our weekly team directors' meeting, when we plan and strategize and do the bulk of the heavy decision making for the organization, and the individual team calls—advocacy, logistics, fundraising and finance, partnerships, media and PR, social media, volunteer intake. I join some of these calls and lead some of them, but mostly the team directors are on it, so it's my job as a leader to support and guide.

I take the Seattle public bus system back home, so all of this is going on with me on my phone and headphones on the bus, riding through downtown Seattle. You could say my natural habitat is the downtown Seattle bus system. It takes me an hour and a half to two hours to bus from school to home. During that time, if I'm not on conference calls or one-on-one calls, I'm listening to music and enjoying the ride through the city. The crisp air, the ocean, the mountains in the distance . . . my happy place is my bus commute where I can look out the window at the Seattle landscape and be reminded of my *why*.

4:30 p.m.: I get home, finally. I usually have more conference calls. I live on video chats and phone calls. Sometimes on these long strings of calls, I don't have time to eat dinner. My mom will occasionally bring cut-up fruit to my "office" (which is a corner of the table in the living room) without me asking for it, which is the sweetest thing ever.

5:00 p.m.: Dinnertime, if it's not one of those back-to-back calls days. We eat at the table, with the TV in the living room talking about some new disturbing news story or trend in American politics. The national news is on 24/7 on my house. So my backdrop is an influx of what disturbing things are happening in the United States. It gets overwhelming, constantly being inundated with news, so sometimes for my sanity as soon as I'm done eating, I blast music through my headphones to take a mental step back for a little while and recharge to pick up the fight again.

5:30 p.m.–8:00 p.m.: It's time to open my computer and get down to business and do all my writing and activism work for the day! I have to ease myself into the work zone, so I usually start by going through emails, then I do all of my conference-call follow-ups, and then I work on the heftier tasks needed for my organization and the climate movement.

8:00 p.m.–10:30 p.m.: Homework, homework, and more homework! I try to finish up everything I have to for the next day.

10:30 p.m.: Time for bed! After pretty much working nonstop for ten hours, I have no brain power to keep going after 10:30. Because most of the work I do is on my computer, my eyes and head hurt a lot by this point in the day. If I stay up working any later than 11:00 p.m., I wake up the next morning with a really bad headache or just fatigue. It's more productive for me to go to bed early even if I don't finish all my homework than to stay up and be miserable the next morning. I leave all my electronic devices in a separate room from where I sleep, so I can properly recharge for the next day.

....**Repeat!**

Obviously, timing looks different on weekends, days I have events, or any other special circumstances. No matter how busy your life as a student is, find ways to work your activism into your schedule!

Daphne Frias, Twenty-One, She/Her

County committee representative; climate justice and disability rights, gun violence prevention, racial justice, anti-gentrification, and anti-gang violence activist; founder of Box the Ballot

JAMIE: **How did you become an activist and a politician?**

DAPHNE: As a disabled woman of color, I have always been an activist because I have had to advocate for myself. I have cerebral palsy. I travel in a wheelchair, and the college process was hard. The school didn't know how to take care of me and my needs, and treated my accommodations as a privilege instead of a necessity, so I stood up for myself.

JAMIE: **How did you decide to take the plunge of running for local office in your community?**

DAPHNE: I live in a predominantly Black and Latinx neighborhood, and it is going through a major shift in gentrification. There has also been a recent rise in gang violence. I am different from the colonizers who have come into my community. I've lived in this neighborhood all my life.

The kickstart for me running for office was my first summer back home from college. I had gotten independence being away from my neighborhood and family, so coming back I saw the community I had grown up in with a fresh perspective. I was floating the idea of running for local office—the community members thought it was a great idea. When I realized that people in my community believed in me and were willing to put their responsibility in me, I went for it.

JAMIE: **What are your strategies for creating change?**

DAPHNE: It's about having people realize that your individual voice does make a difference.

I started an intensive program for people who use reusable water bottles. People who sign on to the campaign get stickers on their bottles that they scan every time they refill, and each scan gives them points. They can redeem those points for a gift card or prize.

JAMIE: **What are your tips for other POC disabled youth who aspire to do/be like you?**

DAPHNE: You have to understand the barriers and obstacles you're coming up against, and then you can plan how to break them down.

JAMIE: **Can you tell us a little more about your nonprofit, Box the Ballot?**

DAPHNE: I started my nonprofit shortly before the 2018 midterms to make sure votes from disenfranchised communities were counted. The purpose was to collect and deliver absentee ballots. There aren't really any clear instructions, and all my friends living on college campuses away from home had trouble figuring it out.

We were able to send over 370,000 ballots to be counted in the 2018 midterms.

MENTAL HEALTH AS AN ACTIVIST

LET'S TALK ABOUT STAYING HEALTHY.

People often think that talking about mental health in activist communities is for oversensitive people who want to overreact to everything and just sit around a fire singing "kumbaya." But it's actually one of the most crucial pillars of being an activist. How are you going to give to your community if you're emotionally empty? I know that sounds cheesy, and trust me, I know where you're coming from.

I'm the kind of girl who used to be like, *Nah, "mental health" and taking care of yourself is for people who don't know how to hustle and get work done…* Then I got so burned out and fed up with everything I wanted to crawl into a hole and never do anything again. I sacrificed too much of my personal life and happiness, so much so that I started resenting the cause. The more unhappy I was, the less productive I became.

After working nonstop for several months, I realized that everything I used to look forward to I dreaded. Conference calls where I got to plan and strategize with my fellow organizers whom I loved? I hated them. Emails and doing daily tasks that used to not bother me at all? It hurt to even log in to my Gmail. That's when I realized, lying there on the couch, hating every bit of the work I used to love, that I was burned out.

Burnout happens when you neglect to take care of yourself and get so invested in your cause that you lose yourself in it in an unhealthy way. Neglecting your mental health as an activist is not a smart move—not for your work, your sanity, or the people around you who will have to put up with your mopey, exhausted self.

Below are tips and reminders for you to always keep at the back (or front) of your mind as you go about your journey as an activist. Not only does following them help you prevent/recover from burnout, but they also just make you happier and more effective in the long run.

THINGS TO ALWAYS REMEMBER THROUGHOUT YOUR ACTIVISM

- **You do not have to be constantly producing and *doing* to be valuable and worthy:** Our worth is often falsely measured by our grades, accolades, and other accomplishments, never by our inherent worthiness and sufficiency of just existing and being ourselves. This feeling of *I am not valuable or worthy if I am not doing and producing 24/7* easily translates into activist spaces and into the way you measure your own worth as an activist. If you are constantly pushing yourself beyond your limits and always *doing* because something in you feels like you owe it to someone or the world to be constantly working yourself to the point of burnout—that's not going to last very long. Your value is not just as an activist of whatever cause you are fighting for—you are also a full person who would be just as wonderful if you weren't an activist.
- **There will always be someone supposedly "better" at what you do than you, and "worse"—comparing yourself to your**

fellow activists and measuring your success against theirs is only going to make you miserable: If you compare your work and accomplishments as an organizer and activist to the work of others, you will never feel like enough, and you will make yourself miserable. There is always, *always,* someone in an objectively "better" position than you (however you measure that) and always someone in a "worse" position. If you make changing the world a contest and measure how well you're doing by how you rank among your fellow activists, you're straying way too far from your *why,* and you're making yourself unhappy.

- **You should never feel guilty about having to take time off to catch up on school, your family, or personal matters:** You are not a bad activist if you have to take a week off to study for an exam, catch up on schoolwork, spend time with your loved ones, or deal with personal issues. That is nothing to feel guilty about. You're not betraying your cause or being selfish by doing so.

- **It's okay to take some time to just be a kid!** You also don't have to have some perfect excuse to take a rest or pull back a little. It doesn't have to be as dramatic as *a close family member died and since I'm planning the funeral I have no choice but to take a few days off and lighten my workload*—it's perfectly valid to take a day off because you want to go to a concert and be a kid! Hang out with your friends, fall in love, watch a movie, do something stupid (but not too stupid). I have found that I bring a much better energy and attitude to my work with my organization and activism all around when I devote some time to doing fun stuff and spending time with the people I love.

- **You have the right to say no and to draw boundaries for yourself:** You don't have to say yes to every opportunity that comes your way! You don't have to be available for your organization, community, or whatever it is you are doing 24/7. In fact, having few to no boundaries is the quickest way to start resenting your activism and getting drained and burned out. Set times for yourself where you do not take calls, answer emails, or do any other work. Make it clear and have people respect those boundaries. For example, you can say, "I'm not doing any work past 8:00 p.m. unless it's a real, actual emergency," or "I will only take four meetings a week, max," or "I won't work on this more than four hours a day." Set them, respect them, have others respect them, and you're going to find yourself so much happier, more energetic, and excited to fight for your cause.

- **Don't be a martyr: sacrificing your health and monetary security for a cause isn't worth it or helpful:** Screw the idea that the only valid way to be an activist is to suffer for your cause. I say, let's change the world but THRIVE while doing it! The amount that you suffer for a cause does not equal how much you care about it or how successful it's going to be. Feeling like a martyr because you are working long hours with little to no pay, feeling like crap all the time, and barely scraping by for your cause is not wise. It doesn't make you superior, effective, or a hero; it just makes you sad. So don't be a martyr—be financially secure, be healthy, have fun, and prioritize your happiness.

TIPS TO DEAL WITH BURNOUT WHEN IT HAPPENS (SOMETIMES IT JUST DOES)

- **Take a breather:** When you're feeling sick of everything, don't put more energy that you don't have into your work. The work you do when you're burned out is not going to be quality work. Take a week or two or more off. Just step away from it all, and take some time to think. Go for walks, hang out with the people you love, and evaluate everything with a fresher mind and perspective.

- **Refocus on what is missing in your life:** A lot of times burnout comes when we've been neglecting ourselves. What is missing in your life? Are you not spending enough time on the hobbies you love? Not enough time with friends and family? Not taking care of your health? Whatever's missing, take some time to refocus on it and give it a lot more attention.

- **Call up people who have been through the same experience as you, and get their tips and advice:** Meet up with fellow activists who understand what you're going through or have a good chat on the phone with them. Just vent about how you're feeling and ask for advice. There's really no medicine for burnout like pouring it all out to a fellow activist who knows exactly how you feel. However, make sure you check in with the person you're going to vent to before you start, to ensure they're in the headspace where they can be receptive and empathetic. Sometimes listening can take a toll.

- **SLEEP:** Get your sleep schedule back on track! Start giving yourself deadlines, like, *No matter what, I'm going to bed before 11:30 every night.* If you're not sleeping well, you're not going to recover as fully and quickly from whatever you're going through.

Aren't used to prioritizing sleep? Now's your time to start. When going through a period of burnout, the best cure is resting up. Now you might be thinking, *Ha, yeah right, I don't have time to sleep.* Well, yes you do. Everyone *has* time, you're just not making time.

You want to know how to start getting into a regular sleep pattern? Set a strict deadline for yourself of, *Even if I haven't finished everything I need to, I am going to bed every weeknight by XYZ time,* and follow it. You'll notice you'll start hustling to finish everything before that deadline and will start getting into a good pattern of feeling healthy and well rested. Pulling all-nighters and then napping a lot is not the same as getting a full eight hours of uninterrupted sleep at night. I'm not a scientist, so I'll let the internet explain how that stuff works if you want to know...but the point is, sleep makes a massive difference.

TIPS FOR AVOIDING BURNOUT

- **Make it a regular habit to #TreatYourself:** There's no shame in taking a break from swimming upstream to get a mani-pedi or be stupid with your friends.

  I don't have to go into detail for this part because it's pretty self-explanatory. Treat yourself. Whatever that means for you. Whether it's giving yourself a makeover, soaking in a bath, going to a place you love...you get it.

  Personally, giving myself a makeover and having a good laugh with my friends is the way I treat myself.

  My friend and Black Lives Matter activist Nupol Kiazolu treats herself by going to the nail salon and getting her nails done. She told me it is her sanctuary, the only way she escapes her crazy life and the craziness of the world. Find your little sanctuaries within your daily life. Small things like getting your nails done are good ways of taking a pause and just being in the moment without stressing about everything on your plate.

  My sanctuary is underneath my headphones. When the music is blasting in my ears, everything becomes a bit more bearable.

  Find your sanctuaries, no matter how little.

- **Participate in therapy and counseling:** I realize this option doesn't work for everyone. Even though it shouldn't be, mental health treatment is often a privilege. Some people do not have the financial resources or insurance plan that affords them a professional therapist. I have friends who display symptoms of clinical depression and anxiety but have parents who don't "believe" in therapy or mental illness or the real effects of trauma, so they don't let them get help. But if therapy is an option for you, I cannot recommend it enough. Of all of the coping and self-care mechanisms, it is the one that has helped me the most. It's important to find a therapist you can vibe with and relate to and who truly understands you. My therapist as of writing this is a young woman I can really open up with. If therapy is something you have the privilege to get, please do. I cannot recommend it enough.

- **Find healthy escapes:** Sure, it's important to be engaged with the world, but to be constantly in that headspace of fighting for your life and your people is exhausting. Sometimes you have to take a break from the real world to recharge and keep going. I sure do. If you struggle with self-medication as a coping tool, reach out to a trusted adult or mentor to help walk you through it.

  These are some healthy escapes that are the only reason I'm still remotely sane:

  » Music: I am the girl with headphones in 24/7. I think if I weren't listening to music all day, I would lose my mind. With the internet it's so easy to find artists who share your struggle and you can relate to. Have you ever lain in a completely pitch-black room with headphones in and just closed your eyes and really *listened* to music? Not had it on kind of playing in the background but really *listened*? My pitch-black-just-listening sessions recharge me and help me calm down and disappear from the world for a bit.

  » TV, theater, and movies: There's nothing like escaping into a good movie or show. When I have the time, I love to hit the movie theater and disappear into the big screen for a bit. It helps put things into perspective and sometimes re-inspires me.

» Netflix and YouTube: I don't think these really need an explanation. Sometimes comfort and a much-needed laugh are just one click away.

» Hanging out with friends and family: There's nothing that gets me feeling good like hanging around the people who get me and make me laugh.

There is no one best coping mechanism; everyone has their strategies that align with their schedules, resources, and passions. Do whatever feels right and works for you.

I hope this helps or at least reminds you that you are a human first, activist second.

Remember: you deserve to make space to care for yourself and be gentle with yourself.

If nothing else motivates you to take care of yourself, let me repeat Audre Lorde's formulation, "Caring for myself is not self-indulgence, it is self-preservation, and that is an act of political warfare."

You are needed in this fight for a better world, and there is no way you can be a useful and productive fighter for change if you do not preserve yourself. It is necessary, radical, and revolutionary to cultivate true self-love in a world that constantly encourages us to hate ourselves and profits from it. This is especially true if you carry identities that our culture teaches us to despise, aim to fix, or view as somehow inherently inferior. It's powerful and revolutionary to love yourself and give yourself permission to help yourself first in a world that demands marginalized people take care of others.

As a young, Jewish, Latina, gay woman, living as my authentic self without shame is an act of resistance. Even if there's no escaping the fact that some people in the world will treat you without kindness, the very least that you can do is show some kindness to yourself. Preserving myself and my health and sanity as a queer woman is vital because the world is built to strike people in my community down. In many parts of the world, LGBTQ+ existence *is* resistance. I always remind myself of that, and I feel a responsibility to be extra proud and authentic for those around the world who cannot.

I have a duty to take a step back and be kinder to myself because the world is already going to be unkind to people like me.

So I guess in a way you never really do take a break from this activist thing...

Greisy Hernandez, Eighteen, She/Her
Founder of Las Chicas Chulas, mental
health advocate

JAMIE: How did you become an advocate for Latinas and mental health for young women of color?

GREISY: I started organizing with the wellness sector at the old General Hospital in LA when I was in middle school. I learned about coping strategies to combat stress and routines to maintain balanced mental health.

Everyone deserves equitable access to mental health services regardless of their race, class, or citizenship status. I struggled with finding resources. You can't pick and choose your struggles, but you can focus on one to create solutions for you and your community.

JAMIE: What is Las Chicas Chulas, and how do you empower and advocate for mental health?

GREISY: I've had a vision of creating a community and safe space for Latinas. This is how Las Chicas Chulas was born. The collective uses social media to help connect folks. I use this platform to uplift conversations on diverse sociopolitical topics, most importantly mental health. We also put on events.

I also ended up using my affinity for fashion to make a Chicas Chulas clothing line, which celebrates melanin and reclaiming Westernized ideas of beauty.

JAMIE: What is your advice to young people on making self-care and mental health a central part in activist space?

GREISY: Self-care is a form of resistance. We need to take care of ourselves and each other so we have the energy to change the world. One of the most practical ways of doing this is by finding your community. There is healing and power in community, especially when we feel safe enough to be vulnerable with each other.

Find a therapist or dedicate a day out of your week to check in with yourself, write your thoughts down, or use the audio recorder on your phone—just rant if you need to! Sometimes we suppress our emotions, and it's really transformative when you hold space for yourself to unpack those emotions. If you use social media, you have the power to curate your feed. Follow mental health experts or people who are optimistic; be intentional with the media you consume.

BUSINESS, MONEY, AND COMPANIES

HOW TO NAVIGATE THE WORLD OF MONEY, BUSINESS, AND COMPANIES AS AN ACTIVIST.

Money and business find their way into everything, including the world of activism.

As a young activist, your power and voice can be very appealing to other organizations, companies, and politicians. A lot of times, especially nowadays with youth activism growing in mainstream popularity, companies recruit young activists to collaborate on ad campaigns and other company initiatives. Organizations will want to use your voice to further their agendas, companies will want to use your voice to sell products, and politicians will want to use your voice to get votes.

None of this is inherently bad. I have worked with other organizations to further agendas I agreed with, worked with a few select environmentally conscious companies, and befriended politicians.

You have to walk a very fine but hard line. Why? Because as young people, we are easy targets to be taken advantage of. I have seen movements and fellow activists get co-opted by corporations, agencies, and very large NGOs that have lost touch with their true cause.

But companies and other entities with large platforms can also help get your message across to a wider audience. The key is that it advances your *why*. If the company or whoever is approaching you to work with you has the same values that you are fighting for, does not conflict with your cause, aligns with your *why*, and would actually help you advance the cause you're fighting for—then that's a good deal, and you should expand your messaging with new opportunities.

But companies will never make themselves seem like they want to use you or make it obvious that their practices conflict with what you are fighting for. They will put their best and friendliest foot forward, so you gotta read the signs and do the research yourself.

Taking a bad deal can be super detrimental for you and the cause you're fighting for. It can make you look like a sell-out, and with selling out comes a loss of power. A young activist's power comes from their untarnished ability to call out the wrongs in this world and speak truth to power. If you suddenly appear hypocritical and water down your powerful message because of a bad guy you've accidentally aligned yourself with, your message will not ring as true anymore. Endorsing a brand that directly conflicts with your *why* and what you're fighting for can drastically hurt you and diminish your power.

Here are some things to remember if a company or other large entity offers you some sort of deal or partnership where you're feeling like *I'm not sure if this is a good deal.*

THINGS TO REMEMBER WHEN CONSIDERING WORKING WITH COMPANIES/LARGE AGENCIES AND ENTITIES

- **Remember why they exist—to make money and sell their products:** Always remember the main mission of the entity reaching out to you. If it's a clothing brand, the reason why they exist is to sell clothes. Sure, they may be sustainable, donate some of their proceeds to women's rights charities—but that is not their main reason for existing. No matter what else they do, their number one purpose is to sell products. Everything else is strategy around building a brand to increase those sales. If a brand is reaching out to you, it's because they think you and the platform you've built can help them sell more of their product. This isn't inherently bad, but it's just important for you to know what you are getting into. Don't walk into a business deal naively. They want something out of you, and that's not always wrong, but it's just a fact. The question to ask is, what can you get out of them back?

- **Think about the long-term impact versus short-term clicks and fame. What is really worth it?** I have been tempted before with opportunities from major companies that drift from my *why* and what I'm actually fighting for but would have given me a lot of short-term fame and social media followers. It would have definitely fed that egotistical part of me that we all have that wants to be recognized, praised, and featured in big places. But when I truly thought about why I'm an activist and what I'm fighting for, I realized that short-term fame was not worth giving up my values and the cause I'm fighting for. If you are being asked to compromise something long term for something flashy and exciting in the short term, ask yourself, *Is this* really *worth it?*
- **Think: Am I (and my message) valuable to them more than this company/opportunity/whatever is valuable to me?** Who would be doing who a favor in this transaction? Is this deal very one sided? Who is the one giving more, and who is more valuable to whom? What companies usually try to do is get you to do more for them than they do for you, while making

you feel like it's such a rare honor to be selected for that "opportunity" that you are willing to compromise.

- **Research their practices, not just what they advertise themselves as:** No company ever is going to put on their website, *We use slave labor and pollute like crazy*... but that doesn't mean they don't. Read on their website what the company says they do, and then consult other reliable sources that are not biased toward or have a responsibility to that company and see what they *actually* do.

HOW TO TELL WHETHER A DEAL IS A GOOD ONE

- **You get just as much in return as they are getting from you:** This goes back to thinking about who is valuable for who. If you are getting just as much from the partnership as the partner is getting from you, that's a good sign. Even better is if you are getting more than they are getting from you. Weigh the labor and favors being asked of you with what is being done for you. If it seems equal or leans more toward helping you, that's a good sign.

- **Their practices align with what you are fighting for:** If after doing your research through reliable, unbiased sources, and they all point to an alignment of the practices of that company with what you are fighting for, that's a good green light. A reliable source could be a recognizable news outlet or research site. If many diverse news sites are saying the same thing, the more likely it is to be true. If it's just one post on Jim-Bob-random-dude's blog that says, *This company is putting chem-trails in the water that are turning all the frogs gay*, chances are that's not a reliable source. You can also check stories on specific fact-checking websites like Snopes.com.

- **They are giving you fair compensation:** Depending on what is being asked of you, there should be some sort of monetary donation to either you or your organization or community in return for your labor, on top of the favors being laid out in the deal. It is not wrong, selfish, or hypocritical to be paid for the speaking engagements, deals, or collaborations you do for another entity. Remember—stay true to your *why*, but don't be a martyr. There is no guilt in being paid for your labor—and there is nothing wrong with asking for—no, *demanding*—compensation if a company clearly has a large budget and can afford it.

Be suspicious of companies that offer you "exposure" and no contract or payment. A lot of times, companies or other entities will try to say something like, *We're not paying you but you get exposure from this opportunity,* as in, they're helping get you more clout. But clout does not usually translate into cash, and you are worth more than just "exposure." If they are a large company that you know can afford to pay you something, saying that they are rewarding you with only exposure is an insult to you and your work, and it's something you should be wary of.

- **They are considerate of your busy life as a student and activist and are not too pushy or demand too much from you:** Partnerships that are worth your trouble will be considerate of your life as a student and not demand unreasonable amounts of work from you that would be a drain on your life. Good partnerships also respect your parents and the adults in your life and have no problem answering questions.

- **They have a history of caring about your cause:** It's also important that whoever is reaching out to collaborate with you as a young activist has a history of advocating for or supporting your cause. If they do, and their interest in you makes sense considering their experience with the same cause, then that is a good sign.

HOW TO TELL WHETHER SOMEONE IS GIVING YOU A BAD DEAL

- **They demand a large amount of labor on your end and are not considerate of your already busy life as a student and an activist:** If the company is demanding unreasonable amounts of work from you, that is a sign they are trying to extract from you, not actually help you. You should never feel overworked, pressured, or have unreasonable standards put on you as a student.

- **They are pushy and do not respect the authority of your parents:** If they are pushy and try to get you to work around your parents or don't want to talk to your parents and answer questions, chances are they are trying to take advantage of you and they don't want an adult in your life to catch that. So walk away.

- **They do not compensate you fairly:** It totally makes sense if a small grassroots organization cannot pay you for a collaboration. But we're not talking about small grassroots organizations. We're talking about big companies and NGOs with massive budgets that could easily afford to pay you for the amount of work you are doing for them. If they refuse to pay you or pay you an amount insufficient for the size of work you're doing for them—they're trying to use you and your voice, and it's time to say *bye-bye!*

- **They do not have a history of caring about and aligning with your cause:** Is a company reaching out to you with no history of actually supporting the cause you work for? That is not necessarily a deal breaker, but it's important to look further into it.

HOW TO SAY NO

So you've come to the conclusion that someone is trying to take advantage of you and your authority and voice as a young activist? It's time to say no. You don't need these people in order to make an impact—you are powerful on your own. Don't be afraid to say no. Don't feel guilty about it. Because the minute you give up on your platform, your whole power as an activist is gone.

Say no firmly but respectfully. Here is a rejection letter, almost verbatim (the actual company name is redacted), that I wrote to a clothing company that wanted me to advertise for them. The company is a big one that I'm sure you've all heard of, but for our purposes I'll just call them "Large Clothing Company."

Hello *Large Clothing Company* Friends,

I have had a lot of conversations with people in the grassroots, my mentors, my family; and while I am so grateful for all the time and consideration you have put in to select me, I have come to the conclusion that being on the *Large Clothing Company* council is not the best fit for me at the time.

I just got the package you sent me and after reading through the contract and what would be required of me, I realized this is a much bigger time commitment than I have space for in my schedule than I initially thought, and there is a lot of advertising for *Large Clothing Company* that you expect from me that I am not comfortable with. I made it clear, I am not comfortable doing any explicit ads selling products of fast fashion, because that goes against my core message of sustainability and defending the environment.

I have so many projects I am working on right now that are taking up a large chunk of my time, and my commitment first and foremost is to the grassroots and protecting the climate.

I cannot go through with being a part of the *Large Clothing Company* youth council.

This is not me closing the door on some sort partnership, however.

I am looking forward to whatever our partnership takes the shape of.... It's just being on the council and representing your company is something I cannot do.

I, however, would be happy to get on a call to talk more about Zero Hour's upcoming actions and your potential sponsorship of them if that is something you're interested in.

Wishing you all the best in finding another young activist to fill my spot on the council.

In Solidarity,
Jamie Margolin

HOW TO SAY YES

- **Get things in writing—CONTRACTS:** You can't take any corporation or nonprofit's word for something. You have to get whatever they are promising in writing, in a contract. This is just how things go. It's not about suspicion or assuming the worst intent; it's just always important to get every transaction you make in writing. Contracts are about making sure everyone's goals and expectations align and all parties are held accountable by clearly delineating the transaction. See a contract as a protection, kind of like insurance for your project. I signed a written contract to publish this book, and the publisher did as well. That way, the transaction between us was outlined clearly, professional expectations were set, and we are both protected. Get every offer, whether it's an ad campaign, a big corporate speaking engagement, or whatever, in writing.

- **Have a trusted adult look over any contract before you sign it:** Never sign or promise a company anything before a trusted adult looks over it. There might be provisions in the fine print of a contract that could really harm you, so make sure a trusted pair of adult eyes okays everything before going ahead.

And that's what you need to know about working with brands, companies, agencies, large nonprofits, politicians, celebrities, or any adult or entity of adults that has a lot of power and wants something from you. There are many great benefits that can come from these collaborations, but being a young person with a message means you are also at risk of being used. Be kind, open, and inviting of opportunities, but take everything with a grain of salt, and approach partnerships carefully.

Remember where your real power comes from, remember your *why*, and don't do anything to compromise them.

Nupol Kiazolu, Nineteen, She/Her
President of Black Lives Matter NYC, fighting institutional racism and police brutality

JAMIE: Can you give me an overview of your story and the work you do?

NUPOL: Trayvon Martin was what got me into activism. I was twelve when he got killed. I decided to hold a silent protest at my school.

I wasn't popular, I was often bullied, so I didn't expect any real impact. I came up with this idea to wear a hoodie and taped to the back of that hoodie, "Do I look suspicious?" and then bought some Skittles and iced tea from 7-Eleven. When Trayvon was murdered, he was unarmed, had Skittles and iced tea, and was wearing a hoodie. The excuse the murderer gave was because Trayvon was wearing a hoodie, it made him look "suspicious."

When I walked into school it caused controversy. The administration wanted me to take the hoodie off. I refused. They threatened me with suspension. I found an ally, my math teacher, a fellow Black woman. She risked her job and came with me to the principal's office with *her* hoodie on and sat there and supported me while I made the case to the school administration.

I came up with a Supreme Court case, *Tinker v. Des Moines*, which granted students' rights to stand up for their political beliefs. I WON. It ended up taking hours.

By the time we got out of the principal's office, it was lunch. We went to the cafeteria, and every student had their hoodies on with the message *"Do I look suspicious?"*

JAMIE: **What are your tips for activists who are just beginning their journey, who want to work with companies and big nonprofits?**

NUPOL: In the beginning, everyone has to go through that phase where you're building your brand. So you can't just come off immediately asking to be paid. You have to be consistent, network. Stay humble.

JAMIE: **What are your tips for how advanced activists should work with companies and large nonprofits?**

NUPOL: I don't do brand and company stuff without being paid, *ever*. My time and talent as an organizer and public speaker are valuable. Adults wouldn't try to shortchange other adults, because they know better. I tell young people to already have your contract, a starting rate for your speaking engagements, and don't waver on it. Know your worth.

Now if it's a community-based thing, I'm not charging. Be subjective, reasonable, and ethical.

16

JEALOUSY, COMPETITION, AND EGO

WHEN THE WORLD DRIVES YOU TO COMPETE AND COMPARE YOURSELF WITH YOUR ALLIES ...

Comparison is the enemy of happiness. In changemaking, comparison is the enemy of achieving what actually matters.

In a field like activism, where so much in our world needs to change and so many people are working to make it happen, it becomes easy to compare yourself and your work to others. Changemaking is not a competition, but we often turn it into one: *They have organized bigger and better events than I have. She has gotten so much more attention for her activism. They've made a much bigger impact on the world than I have!*

For those of us with large ambitions combined with a lack of self-confidence and self-worth, it can be far too tempting to fall into the trap of feeling like our own work is not enough. We are all humans, and humans have egos. We tend to let our egos cloud our judgment of what really matters and fill us with greed and envy of others who are on our same team, fighting for the same cause. Especially in today's world, where more fame, funding, and social media followers often means having a larger reach and impact, it's easy to resent other activists for having the power of a public figure that some of us long for.

Sometimes that little voice telling you *I should be getting more recognition for my work* is totally right. If you're someone on the front lines of an issue, if you're an activist from a marginalized community who has been doing really hard work for a long time, your work *should* be paid more attention. Your voice is not heard enough in our society, and it's important that you keep working to make sure your community's needs are met.

So when I talk about letting go of our egos in this chapter, I don't mean stop fighting for your voice to be listened to more. I mean that it's time to free ourselves of our resentment and jealousy of others, because those feelings only hold us back from our goals.

I have spent more hours than I'd like to admit scrolling through social media and feeling bitter and self-righteous toward my fellow activists, comparing myself to them and longing for what others had. I carry a lot of unhappiness that I often try to fill with external validation, so yes, sometimes it makes me feel like crap. As a social media addict in a world that pits people against each other for accolades, it's pretty easy to fall into that trap of egotistical self-deprecation when looking at what others have accomplished in comparison to yourself.

To overcome things like comparison, competition, insecurity, or jealousy toward our fellow activists, we have to acknowledge those feelings. Ego, envy, resentment, or entitlement over someone else's success are super damaging in movement spaces. They undermine relationships and our ability to work with others, which are crucial to making change. Those negative feelings cloud our decision-making abilities and often lead us to taking empty, clout-chasing, flashy actions that add no value to what we are trying to change in the world. Often, that blind clout chasing just makes the problem worse. Those feelings also just make you miserable. Jealousy makes you lose sight of your own worth, where you are in your own journey. Ever since I was little, my mom always told me that the only thing comparing myself to others would accomplish is making me vain and unhappy. Resenting others doesn't help you get ahead; it slows you down from going where you want to go.

So now that we've admitted to ourselves that feelings like these exist in our movements and that they are not good or productive for the greater good, let's talk about getting past them.

How do we get over ourselves?

STEPS TO OVERCOMING EGO/JEALOUSY/COMPETITION AMONG OUR ALLIES

1. **Acknowledge how you're feeling:** It's perfectly valid and okay to just stop and be like, *Even though I should be happy for this other young person who is fighting for the same thing I am, I am feeling really envious of all the attention and platform they're getting after just starting their activism, when I have been doing this work for years and no one has paid attention.* Yeah, it sucks. You're allowed to feel that and admit it to yourself.

   Especially if you are a young indigenous organizer or organizer of color who has been doing work for a while, and then white kids just start working on something and it blows up immediately, while your work is still ignored. This has happened and keeps happening in pretty much every single movement I can think of, from gun reform to climate justice. Over and *over* again. It's totally unfair, and it's okay to be bummed about that.

   Let yourself feel your feelings, but don't publicly act on them! Don't go hating on those organizers you're jealous of on social media, making enemies, or lashing out. You will regret it, and it does nothing for the greater good. Do not break down your fellow organizers! We are all on each other's side.

Instead, I recommend my tried-and-true method—calling up someone who feels the same and just complaining about how you feel to each other. Get it all out. Call up fellow activists and just vent until you've gotten it all out of your system.

No public social media diatribes, no making enemies, no damaging the movement, no hating on the new privileged activists who are suddenly getting all the press, just good old harmless venting with someone on the same page as you.

2. **Remind yourself of your *why*:** Now that you've gotten all that ego, entitlement, envy, or whatever it is you're feeling out of your system, it's time to recenter. First, let's remind ourselves what activism is *not* about. Activism isn't about ownership or credit. It's not about who gave who a head start. It's not about who gets the most clout, who can be the most publicly enlightened and "woke." It's not about who did what first, who should be getting credit for what, who has the most press, who has the coolest speaking engagements, who has the most social media followers, who gets the most funding.

What *is* it about?

Well that is something different for each of us. You defined what it means to you when you discovered your *why* (see Chapter 1). It is important for us to set rituals and practices in place that remind us to stay grounded in why we're really doing this work. Twenty-one-year-old youth activist and elected official Daphne Frias has a great method for remembering your *why:*

Every month I set time aside to make little vision boards of photos and things that remind me of what I've accomplished and where I want to go.

I have one original vision board I made at the beginning of my journey. It is all about who I am, my community, and who I am fighting for. The vision board has pictures of my family, my dog, my community, and victims of gun violence. My core. I recommend everyone make a vision board or something of that sort of who you are at your core. Who and what you love, exactly what you are fighting for.

So every month, when I'm re-grounding and making my monthly vision boards, I reflect on my old one and make sure I'm still true to it. In that process of cutting and pasting and making those monthly vision boards, I have time to think and reflect on how my activism is or is not consistent with my original vision board:

Am I staying true to my community? Am I staying true to what I fight for? Am I staying true to who I am as a person and my values?

Those reflection days are so important for me. Grounding yourself as an activist is crucial. It's important to integrate practices in your life that regularly remind you *this is who I am as a person, this is what I'm fighting for, and this is who I advocate for and represent.*

It's all about perspective. Taking time to reflect on what I have accomplished helps keep me from falling into that trap of wishing we had other people's capsulized Instagram lives that always look so much better than our own. Not only does this exercise make you a more genuine activist, it also makes you realize, *I'm really amazing too!* I feel like these days we need a reminder that it's okay to be proud of yourself. It's okay to tell yourself that you are enough. You don't have to be constantly striving for more every minute of every day.

Try that the next time you're feeling bogged down by jealousy or competition or just feeling discouraged and disconnected to your *why.*

3. **Identify the causes for these bad feelings and reduce exposing yourself to them as much as possible:** Are there specific things that you do or places you go that trigger that insecure, jealous part of yourself?

   For me, it's social media. Social media is necessary to the work I do and to the work many young activists do, but for me there are times when it has gone too far and kind of hijacked my mind. I get easily addicted, and I go through periods when social media takes up way more space in my mind and time than it should. Looking at other people's lives and accomplishments on social media often puts me in comparison mode and makes me feel like the work I've been doing is insignificant. It's very easy for me to descend into that rabbit hole of comparing myself to others, so I limit my social media time as much as possible. I set time limits on my phone for social networking apps and sometimes even just delete the Instagram and Twitter apps from my phone for a few days when I need to get away from that constant temptation of the instant gratification social media offers. Find out what triggers your unhealthy feelings, and avoid or find healthy ways to cope with them as much as possible!

4. **Go to places that make you happy and remind you of your *why*:** Hang out with people or pets, and go to the places that remind you that all that superficial stuff and your negative ideas about yourself and your activism don't actually matter in the long run.

   Spend time with the members of your community you are trying to help. I notice that when I talk to people on the front lines of the climate crisis or go out in nature to the beautiful places of the Pacific Northwest that I am fighting to protect, my obsession over the superficial aspects of activism seems silly.

I look out at the acidifying Pacific Ocean, and I realize it doesn't give a damn how many news articles have been written about me. The starving, dying orcas don't care about how many social media followers I have. That doesn't help them.

When I am out in nature, I realize that awards and accolades...those are all just social constructs humans made up and assigned fake value to. We take pictures of each other and call each other heroes and interview each other while the world burns. But the air we breathe, the water we drink, the beautiful places of our earth, the people we fight for—they aren't social constructs. They have real value.

So I go down to the park by the beach near my house whenever I am feeling consumed by the superficial pressures, and it reminds me why I'm actually doing what I do.

Spend time with those who would not be the slightest bit impressed if you got crazy-famous from your activism. The people, places, and things you are actually fighting to protect. Take some time to put things into context. It actually helps quite a bit.

5. **Take time to be proud of your own accomplishments and acknowledge how far you have come on your own path:** Remember—you are allowed to be happy with yourself! You're allowed to be proud of what you have accomplished, no matter how small. You're allowed to celebrate your wins and take a breather every so often. Usually, resentment builds when we have drowned ourselves so deep in the cause that we have burned out. I have noticed my negative feelings about my activism materialize when I have been neglecting myself. Ninety-nine percent of the time I'm not genuinely resentful of my fellow activists; what I actually am is tired or dealing with some bad stuff in my life, and I'm projecting that onto others. When I am overworked, tired, not taking care of myself, and

putting way too much pressure on myself is when I develop insecurities around others. When I dig deep, I realize that I don't actually *want* all that superficial stuff, I'm just trying to fill some deeper emotional hole with instant gratification, hoping maybe the next high of external validation will finally make me truly happy and confident in my activism. Spoiler alert: it never does.

Maybe your feelings of insecurity stem from the way you are working. So slow down, take a deep breath, and take care of yourself! And give yourself a pat on the back for all you've done already. It's not easy swimming upstream in this world, but you're doing it, and if you aren't told that you're enough in your daily life—this is me telling you that you are enough! The work you do is enough. You are good enough, and you are kick-ass!

Tokata Iron Eyes, Sixteen, She/Her
#NoDakotaAccessPipeline Standing Rock
movement founder, Water Protector

JAMIE: Tell me what your activism journey has been like!

TOKATA: I got started when I was nine. It was the first time
I ever spoke in public. Before that, activism was about
being raised within my indigenous culture and being
taught outside the Western education system. In 2016, the
No Dakota Access Pipeline fight took over my life. When
I was twelve I found out it was going to be built right next
to my community! I was disrupted from being a kid to
fight this pipeline. I lived in Standing Rock, North Dakota,
an indigenous reservation. There, privilege is having a
roof over your head, two parents, and never being scared.
It made me think about the other kids in my community
who also cared but didn't have the resources to speak
up. I decided to use mine to speak up and stand against
the pipeline. This was treaty land, so indigenous people
decided to occupy it as a physical sign of resistance,
blocking the pipeline construction and harnessing this
indigenous system and way of life and values. We hosted
nonviolent direct actions almost every day; #NoDAPL was
an occupation in prayer and ceremony.

**JAMIE: How do you stay true to your cause and keep your
organizing spaces free of competition and ego?**

TOKATA: When you're talking about changing something huge, a lot of times, when we start to get notoriety, we lose our intention. Being able to really connect with each other and the cause is crucial. If you put up false personas to the people you work with, then you give false signals to those who trust you. Be conscious of your words and what they mean to other people. Reach out to those who are indifferent and access them and the things that make them want to create change. When we're surrounded by people who always think the same, we forget we're fighting for those who don't. Recognize that there are already thousands of people doing the same work in their communities. We need to create solutions that are diverse and accessible.

JAMIE: What are some practices that the rest of the activist movement could learn from indigenous organizers?

TOKATA: Relearn this connection to nature. I grew up knowing that nature was my relative and everything in it was a part of me. People only fight for something they feel affects them, but if you learn how we are all connected with nature and each other, one person's suffering is our collected suffering. It's not the earth's suffering, it's all of our suffering.

17

BUILDING A COMMUNITY TO CHANGE THE WORLD

THE ANTIDOTE TO HOPELESSNESS IS NOT JUST ACTION BUT COMMUNITY.

The biggest lie you can be told about changemaking in any cause is that change can be achieved alone. To overcome the systems and laws that oppress us, to build a better world, we need community. We need as many people as possible pushing the needle toward change. Now, the word "community" may sound broad to you, so let's narrow it down to the community you work in. The organization, neighborhood group, or movement that you do your justice work with. It is actually just as useful and important to the cause that you live out the values you are fighting for inside your organization or movement as it is for you to advocate for those values on the outside. How are you going to dismantle the world's systems of oppression if you perpetuate them within your own organization? How are you going to advocate for a more compassionate, fair, democratic, kind, and functional world if you are not fair, democratic, kind, and functional within your own organization? The space that you work in and the environment that you cultivate within your movement is so incredibly important, it's worth investing time and resources into bettering.

First of all, infighting and internal conflict within organizations can bring down movements and make you a lot weaker in the face of your opponents. Let's be honest (and I'll use the climate justice movement as an example), the oil, gas, mass industrial farming, and chemical industries have money, political power, and pretty much all the resources on their side. They are literally a well-oiled machine. We, the scrappy activists preventing them from ending all life on earth as we know it, don't have much going for us except the fact that we outnumber them. But the only way we can leverage that fact is with unity and organized strategy, community, public pressure, and smart tactics. If that strategy, community, and unity is disrupted, well, the movement isn't going to go very far, and we're not going to fare well against a literally well-oiled machine with so much cash they don't know what to do with it.

As changemakers, we can't afford infighting. We can't afford to claim to stand for justice, fairness, equality, and change when the environments we work in are unjust, unequal, or toxic. I'm saying this because I've seen organizations (this very much includes organizations run by young people) get so caught up with the external work and pressures that we neglect the internal upkeep and community building. Building community is half of this whole changemaking thing.

So let's cultivate some amazing movement spaces!

This is easier said than done, because—let's be honest—working with other humans is hard! Movements and organizations don't fall into infighting and dysfunction because we hate each other and don't care about our community. It's because it takes a lot of work, practice, learning, and emotional labor to be properly in touch with the people we work with. Taking care of each other as we fight for a better world is half of living out that better world that we want to create, but it's super hard!

People have feelings, can be really bad at communicating their feelings, and have different opinions than you. Humans are annoying—I'm just going to lay it out there. I don't always enjoy us. We require constant upkeep and checking in, and there are these annoying things like *mental health* and *work/life balance* and *boundaries* that need to be upheld (such a pain!).

Ideas can be misunderstood and miscommunicated (especially when it comes to long-distance digital organizing), and strong clashes of opinion, or just plain old ego and unresolved internal issues, can get in the way of progress.

If you are struggling with conflict either within your organization/community/movement or with another organization/community/movement—welcome to the club. People are annoying and difficult, but working with other humans unfortunately is crucial for our success as activists.

If you are in the trenches of conflict within your own organization or with other organizers/organizations... well, first of all I want to give you a big hug. That stuff sucks! But let's stop feeling sorry for ourselves and fix this and build a better community for all of us! Here are my best tips for dealing with any conflict that has arisen in your movement.

THE ULTIMATE GUIDE TO HAVING AN AMAZING COMMUNITY/ORGANIZATION WHERE PEOPLE ACTUALLY LIKE EACH OTHER AND GET ALONG AND ARE FUNCTIONAL

1. **Bring it up! Don't expect people to read minds:** It's important to never assume that the people you work with know

how you are feeling and what you are thinking. I have been in so many situations where people have had problems with the way I lead, work, whatever, but they never actually said anything about it. They dropped hints and expected me to read their minds. I didn't pick up on their indirect cues, so resentment and hostility about buried issues would build up over time until finally they exploded in everyone's faces.

So many problems could have been prevented or resolved much sooner if people just told me directly what the problem was. Moral of the story? If there is something in your movement space that is bothering you or if you have a problem with someone or an organization, bring it up to them directly. Don't gossip behind people's backs. Don't post passive-aggressive things about them on social media. In fact, skip the passive-aggressiveness and pettiness all together.

Got a problem? Bring it up professionally and directly to the person you have an issue with. Don't do it in front of everyone.

Scared of confrontation or bringing up issues to people? Either just grit your teeth and push past it or get a trusted member of your organization to help bring it up with you. I understand some people have social anxiety and other conditions that make direct communication hard, so do whatever is best for you, whether that be a *professional* email airing grievances (please, no aggressive email writing while you are in the heat of emotion—that never goes well), a facilitated meeting, or whatever works best for you.

If there is a serious power imbalance between you and the person you need to talk to (say you're bringing a problem to a boss who decides your pay check or you are a young woman of color student bringing a problem to an older white male professor), find a powerful ally to help you bring the problem up.

Some examples of good communication and conversation starters:

Hey! I love working with you, but there have been a few things in our workspace bothering me that I'd like to talk about with you sometime...

I love being in this movement with you, which is why we need to chat about ways to improve the current way we're working, because some things have been bothering me...

I should also add that direct and clear communication with the person you need to air grievances with should not be made into a public spectacle. If you cc a bunch of other people on your email, it is no longer personal. You are causing a scene and communicating that you are not there to get that person to change but rather doing a sort of self-righteous public callout. Performative fake wokeness helps no one. It makes people defensive and less inclined to listen to you. It forces everyone witnessing the moment to choose sides. It makes a mess. Take it from someone who has made these messes before.

Use your common sense and put yourself in their shoes. If someone were bringing up a problem or concern to you, which way of being approached would you be most receptive to?

2. **Get a facilitator and invest in workshops and trainings:** An outside professional perspective can be super important, not just for conflict mediation but for the general betterment of your organization and movement. Many organizations have annual retreats facilitated by nonprofit and intersectional justice professionals who help them work on their team dynamics, strategy, and interpersonal communication.

A quick internet search and just talking to organizers who have been in the field for a while can generate some names of great facilitators and organizations who can take your interpersonal work to the next level.

But you don't have to take it that far, and I realize that this is not necessary or accessible for most of us students just trying to juggle our lives the best we can!

So my tip for you is to really just find someone completely neutral to the situation who is willing to facilitate a conversation between the parties having the conflict. It can be an activist from a different organization, a mentor, or someone within your organization who is impartial. Whoever it is, it can't be someone who has a bias toward one person or another. Having an impartial mediator has helped me and other organizers I know work through issues and move forward: 10/10 would recommend!

3. **Install infrastructure in your organization that provides a democratic process of organizing and voting:** In my experience, there are typically two main types of people in movement spaces: the people who talk all the time and are very open about their opinions and the people who stay quiet, let the verbal people have their way most of the time, and have to have their thoughts painfully pried out of them.

You know what kind of people *don't* exist in organizing spaces, though? People with no opinions. If they say they don't care, chances are they're not revealing something to you. Everyone has an opinion when it comes to large decisions, and I have had the aggravating experience over and over again of people staying quiet as the decision is made and then afterward grumpily expressing their disdain for the outcome.

This is why it's crucial to have a system in place that forces people to raise their voices and make it clear what they want. Spend some time creating infrastructure for your organization that clearly lays out a democratic decision-making process. In that system make sure no one is allowed to opt out of basic communication. Having systems in place that ensure people communicate and have their opinions and concerns valued creates a culture of democracy and open communication, which is crucial to successful organizing.

It is also crucial to ensure that the most marginalized and silenced voices in your group are heard. There cannot be one or a few people doing most of the talking and decision making in a large group. Rules and procedures that normalize listening to everyone and giving everyone a voice make the whole process a lot more empowering and effective for everyone.

Also, if you are one of those people who doesn't voice your concern in meetings or keeps your important opinions to yourself . . . it's time to stop expecting people to read your mind! Not only is it important to make systems that encourage democratic and equal participation, but the people in that group have to be willing to participate and not put the unfair burden of mind reading on everyone else.

4. **Assess everyone's visions for your movement/organization and see whether they clash:** Remember, conflict happens in movement spaces, but there are different levels of dysfunction. An especially high dysfunction level within your organization or space for an extended period of time may be an indicator of a larger problem.

Does everyone in your organization/movement have a similar overall goal and vision? Or are there some key fundamental, strategic, and ideological conflicts that are driving the organization apart? Is there a major ideological divide? Is the majority of your organization not thrilled about the direction you're going?

Direct communication and confronting the main issues are key here. Be the brave one to bring it up to your team—*Do we all have the same strategy for changemaking? Do we all actually want to do this thing we've been working on for so long? Does everyone still want to be here? Is this the cause for everyone here?*

Have a meeting or call where people share their honest thoughts and opinions about the way the movement is going. Oftentimes, these big-picture differences are what fuel the everyday small conflicts.

I know because this has happened to me. Oh, the long nights and stress that could have been avoided if people just practiced direct communication and advocated for themselves instead of expecting people to read their minds . . . **sigh**

I admit I have cultivated spaces before where not everyone has felt heard and people didn't like the direction I was taking them. The problem was that no one actually told me this until after they had let the problem build up, so by the time they talked to me, it was a laundry list of complaints of things I'd been doing over the span of a whole year. I love constructive feedback and am open to learning and growing, but we can only learn and grow if someone tells us that we need to!

5. **Reflect on whether you are in the best space for the work you want to do and whether the space is changeable:** Sometimes conflict comes from realizing that the space you're organizing in is not the right one for you. So take some time to reflect on the situation. Is it the right place for you? Do you feel safe, appreciated, and empowered in the space you're organizing in? Has the conflict been going on for a long time? Is there an end to the problems in sight? Can the trouble be fixed, or is this something that's not going away anytime soon? What would be better for you and the movement—staying and fighting it out or finding a different home for your work?

Take a few weeks to mull over these questions and really just be honest with yourself.

6. **No matter what is happening, don't let activism drama take over the rest of your life. Period. No exceptions:** I have made the mistake of doing this before. My organization was going through a turbulent transitional period, and it was a living hell for about three weeks. Those three weeks felt like months, and every day was a horrible emotional roller-coaster. It felt like everything I had worked so hard for was falling apart before my eyes. I had given up pretty much everything else in my life for the cause (not a healthy way of being an activist, FYI), and now everything was falling through. I felt betrayed by people I had previously trusted, and things that I thought were set in stone were suddenly not so certain. I was supposed to be studying for midterm exams, but I neglected my schoolwork to dive headfirst into solving our issues. Every time I thought the problem was resolved, an ugly surprise would blindside me, and I'd be back in the trenches, trying to hold everything together by a thread.

For those three weeks I ignored and stressed out my family. I completely neglected my friends and let them down on several occasions, spending more time on my phone than with the people who would love me no matter what happened to Zero Hour. I stopped taking care of myself. I neglected school and ended up doing worse than I'd ever done before. I let the rough patch my organization was going through completely take over my life.

Eventually we at Zero Hour resolved these internal problems, and we have all learned so much and are better for it.

So what's the point of this story? The point is, don't do what I did. Don't drop everything else in your life to save whatever is happening with your activism. Don't let whatever drama, conflict, or hardship going on with your organization or activism take over the other parts of your life. It's not worth it, and incidentally, drowning yourself in your activist problems only makes things worse. If you don't take time to breathe, be with the people or pets you love, and get in touch with the other parts of your identity outside your cause, you will be angrier and more impatient when trying to resolve the conflict, which will just make it worse.

So there you have it! My tips and advice on dealing with the realities of working toward a hard goal with other human beings.

I have learned so much (the hard way) about interorganizational conflict and come out the other side of it stronger and a much better and fairer activist and organizer. It took years of trial and error before finally finding a system that worked and starting to understand the dynamics of working with other people. And I still mess up sometimes, and I'm still learning!

MISTAKES I'VE MADE THAT I KEEP SEEING OTHER YOUTH MOVEMENTS MAKE AGAIN AND AGAIN . . . AND HOW TO FIX THEM!

1. **Dictatorships:** I used to kind of be a dictator very early on in my leadership of Zero Hour, and that made the work experience within our organization not so great for some people. There was no democratic institutional system of decision making. I was the one with the power, and it was either my way or the highway. It didn't happen consciously where I was like, *I'm going to make everyone else's working experience miserable and call all the shots myself.* I just wanted what I thought was best for the movement, and believe it or not, I didn't notice that I was behaving very much like a dictator and that a lot of people were upset about it. I didn't notice it was getting in the way of

the movement until a few people held a literal intervention. But we at Zero Hour overcame it. I gained a lot more self-awareness and awareness of other people's needs and feelings; we installed fair, democratic systems for consensus-based decision making; and everyone learned from that experience. My dictator days (I would like to think) are behind me.

So it's time we learn from each other's mistakes. Take some time to reflect. Is your workspace fair and democratic? Is there one person or a few people with way too much power calling the shots for everyone?

The solution: Gather everyone in your group, and cultivate a space to talk openly about what is going on. Set some ground rules around respect and letting each person voice their opinion and air out their grievances of how the organization or movement is being run. Outline on a document the main things that need to change, and start to put together a more democratic system where everyone's needs and ideas are equally weighed. It's worth looking at other democratically run organizations and movements for inspiration. Observe their structures and decision-making processes, and see where you can apply what they are doing to improve your space. We're young, we're all learning, so there's no need for excessive guilt or self-deprecation when you realize that things need to change within your movement. Just be open to learning, changing, and making the environment you work in one that you are fighting to make the world like: fair, democratic, and inclusive.

2. **Neglect of team dynamics:** I used to always neglect the social, interpersonal part of organizing. I would be hesitant and stingy when it came to allocating time and resources to issues like trainings, facilitators, and making sure the social environment was safe and welcoming for everyone. I would just be like, *Okay let's get down to business. Why are we wasting time with*

people's feelings? We have a job to do! That meant a lot of issues built up and blew up in our faces because there was no outlet for improving our organizational team dynamics and inter-personal communication.

The solution: Spend time and resources in working on team dynamics and the internal operations of your organiza-tion or movement. Take the time to do some training or even just have open conversations with those you work with about improving your workplace. Give people space to be humans, not just robots churning out work for the movement. Always make sure to dedicate time to working on the interpersonal parts of our organizing—not just cranking out the work. This can mean activities where everyone just chills and hangs out together, specific healing and interpersonal work trainings, fa-cilitated discussions, and the like.

3. **Giving responsibility to those who have proved they're not responsible:** So many times, I have kept people around who proved that they were incapable of or just not going to do the work in their positions. I have let incompetent, unmoti-vated, and irresponsible workers keep their jobs and talk me out of replacing them. My fear of confrontation and hurting people's feelings has cost my movement a lot of money, time, and success. Letting people keep positions they have no inten-tion of honoring sabotages the movement. Delegating work to those who don't follow through is a recipe for disaster. This is a sensitive topic, because it can be difficult to weigh which people don't care versus which people just work differently or mean well but don't have the skills for the job.

The solution: Take it on a case-by-case basis and let the person know the issues you are having so they can give you their side of the story. Try to find solutions that work for them as well as for the good of the organization.

Bottom line, when people show you who they are—*believe them*. Don't keep giving them third, fourth, fifth, tenth, twentieth chances when they proved a few times over that they're not going to be responsible.

4. **Parental involvement:** There's been a rise in activist "stage moms," in other words, helicopter parents focused on getting their kids famous for being activists...which is so twisted, because the goal of being an activist should be to drive change, not become famous. If that is what you want and expect from your activism, take a step back and reflect on whether this work is really for you. Fame for being an activist is not only rare and unglamorous, but the work-to-fame ratio is like a hundred hours of work for fifteen seconds of minor fame. If your goal in life is to be famous, I suggest doing something else, like going viral for saying something dumb on the internet.

Anyway, these activist stage moms get in the way of their kids' relationship building and their general activism, and they often lash out at other activists' parents (or even other young activists) complaining, *Your kid is hogging all the press! Why was your kid in the* New York Times *for XYZ—and mine wasn't!?*

Not only do you have to put your own ego in check as an activist; you also need to make sure your parents' egos do not take over or interfere with your work. The extent of my mom's involvement with my activism? She sometimes brings me cut-up papaya when I'm on a conference call for too long, makes sure I'm safe when I'm doing events away from home, and sometimes comes along on speaking trips to keep me company and take pictures. The extent of my dad's involvement with my activism? He helps me look over contracts so I don't get screwed over, manages my schedule with different engagements, gives consent for things like interviews that need parental sign off, helps out with manual labor at some of Zero Hour's events, makes sure I'm safe when I'm doing events away from home, and sometimes provides me transportation for close-to-home events. And that's it. Sometimes they try to get more involved, but I draw the line and do not let them, because my parents are not organizers nor do they have any movement experience, so they might do more harm than good.

The solution: Here's the general rule of thumb: parental involvement in your activism should be to keep you safe—look over contracts, schedule, logistics of your physical well-being, and make sure no one is exploiting or taking advantage of you. Their job as much as possible is to be your parent, not your publicist. No, your mom cannot call up some other activist's mom and complain about how her kid doesn't get as much notoriety as theirs. No, your dad cannot take over a conference call if he has no involvement with the organization and is just there to insert his out-of-context opinion.

Obviously there are different situations where this rule can be bent for youth with special needs or in unique circumstances—but the bottom line is, too much parental involvement, especially egotistical involvement, ruins youth movements.

It's one thing if your parents are also activists, you are starting an organization with them, or you are working on a cause as a family. That's fine—in fact, intergenerational community organizing is a beautiful thing and results in a lot of great progress. What you want to avoid is parents who have no background in activism or any real knowledge of the field you're working in taking over to be a stage parent and leaning too much on the ego side.

While doing your best to avoid the mistakes above, also be compassionate with yourself, and know that no matter how hard you try, mistakes will happen. Life is busy and chaotic, and things get forgotten or go unnoticed.

If you are a perfectionist and live your life in fear of making mistakes, you will not get far, because you are restricting your ability to grow and explore as an activist. There is a problem in the activist community of "cancel culture" and "performative wokeness," where everyone tries to one-up each other on how non-problematic they are and never lets anyone recover from a mistake. Essentially, the minute you slip up, you're "canceled," and that kind of attitude needs to stop within activist spaces. If you have made any of the above mistakes or more, that doesn't make you a bad person or activist. It doesn't make you a failure. It's just something you need to work on. It is so difficult just trying to grow up, be a young person, and navigate this crazy world and your path in it, all while being a student, dealing with social pressures, *and* fighting to change the world. Craziness is bound to happen. So when it does, acknowledge it, correct it, learn from it, but don't beat yourself up for it. You're still growing and learning—so allow yourself that space.

Iris Fen Gillingham, Nineteen, She/Her
Climate justice activist, Growing Wildroots Farm

JAMIE: **How did you become an activist?**

IRIS: First, the way that I was raised, on my family's organic farm. I was named after a flower in the wetland, which made me feel a connection and certain responsibility to work with the earth. When I was six, my family, who had been making a living growing organic vegetables, experienced two 100-year floods and one 500-year flood within the span of five years. It washed away all of the topsoil. We still live off the grid and grow our own food, but we were forced to stop making our living off of selling vegetables. When I was eight the fracking industry came into my community. I grew up with a dad who was working nonstop to fight fracking and protect the place that I love. As I got older, I began speaking out. All the adults said they were doing this for their kids and grandkids, but I was the only young person in the room. For a while, life was taken over by climate change activism with many organizations. Now, I focus on the aspect of self-care in activism and how we walk on the earth a little more gently, taking responsibility for the earth and our action.

JAMIE: **What needs to change within movement spaces?**

IRIS: We often focus on the products and don't acknowledge the value of process and journey. With many of the groups I've worked with, I've seen so many times how health, care, and relationships have been put second. What should be first is the community and support we need to be giving each other.

JAMIE: **How do we create community in activism?**

IRIS: Support each other. Be a family. When one of our sisters or brothers is on the front lines, we're right there with them. Not just a Twitter shout-out—we're literally right there with them.

What we're doing is listening to communities on the front lines, what kind of support and allyship they need. We surround ourselves with people that lift us up and don't pull us down.

The power of youth is we don't just say what we want to say; we say what's in our hearts.

Each of us have individual strengths, and we need to keep that candle burning. Having the ability to be a part of that community is amazing, and we can start to create that by following our hearts and doing what we love.

18

STANDING ON THE SHOULDERS OF GIANTS AND MOVING FORWARD

TAKING YOUR SKILLS AS A YOUTH ACTIVIST TO BUILD AN INTERGENERATIONAL MOVEMENT FOR CHANGE.

You are a part of a global family of changemakers that has been slowly but surely bending the moral arc of the universe toward justice for centuries. Among all the hard work and nitty-gritty of our individual lives, it can become easy to forget that we are each a puzzle piece in a movement that has existed long before us. We are a part of something bigger than ourselves. We are a part of a community; we are no longer one of the many gears turning in society's machine. Being an activist and daring to challenge what the world lays in front of you as "the only way it will ever be" has broken you free. It's time to use your skills as a young organizer and build an intergenerational movement for change—because that is the only way we will win.

We live in a world where justice is never simply handed over. It has to be demanded, and then demanded over and over again. For every great social movement in history, it has taken the unique wisdom and strength of every generation united to move the needle toward change.

Youth to Power is not about elevating the younger generations over the older ones, because the truth is, we are all standing on the shoulders of the changemakers who came before us. The current environmental movement is standing on the shoulders of indigenous activists who have been fighting to protect the earth and humanity's relationship to it from colonial greed and destruction for centuries, the current LGBTQ+ liberation movement is standing on the shoulders of queer activists who rioted at Stonewall in the late 1960s, and on and on. We get nowhere by alienating ourselves from our elders, but we also have to make sure those who deny our value are corrected. We must pull up a seat to the table for young voices, because usually no one will pull up a seat for us.

Youth movements don't get anywhere by alienating and making enemies out of our elders, in the same way that movements with little to no youth voice involved or considered are never successful in truly serving justice for everyone.

You are existing right now in a crucial moment in history. The decisions you make, the action you take as a young person in the twenty-first century with a voice and strong convictions will shape the world for thousands of years to come. The action you take now will decide the future of our planet and everything on it. Maybe we the youth do not have much of the institutional, legislative, media, legal, or monetary power in this world—but we have the power to influence and speak the truth to each and every one of these systems of power.

You as a young person in today's world have something important to say, something special to offer society. Our power, the power of young people, is the power to speak the pure, undiluted truth to those in high places. Young people may not control our world's political systems, but we have a massive influence on our world's culture, and cultural shifts cause political shifts. Before a law can change, the culture surrounding the society that creates those laws needs to change. Youth have and always will steer our society's culture toward progress. That is our power. That is our job. That is our gift.

This is the end of this book but only the very beginning of your journey. *Youth to Power* is not just a catchy title or hashtag. It's a way of existing in the world as a young person, being both a force of resistance against the oppressive forms of power in the world and a force of change bringing power to the values, systems, and people that need it. It's time to live out *youth to power* in all its forms. Be the one who stands up and speaks truth to power, even when it is difficult and unpopular. Be the one who draws the line and says, *No more.* No more destruction of our environment and planet, no more violence in our communities, no more discrimination based on race, gender, ethnicity, sexuality, religion, or ability. Be the one who dares to imagine and create better possibilities, solutions, and ways of living in place of those old systems that have only harmed us. Be the one who laughs in the face of those who say, *But it's ALWAYS been this way,* and create something that disrupts the status quo in the best way possible. Because why *not* you? It isn't rare for many people to have the same yearning to be free and the same concerns and dreams of a better world that you have, but they are waiting for someone to be the first person to stand up and speak for it. Years can go by where no one says anything or those who do don't say enough— so you just have to stand up and decide, *enough already,* and be the one to break the silence. Then those who have felt that way all along will follow.

This journey as a young changemaker is going to be long, crazy, confusing, wonderful, empowering, disappointing, thrilling, exhausting, energizing, beautiful, and *so* worth it.

There is absolutely no feeling in the world better than knowing you are fighting for what is right and actually doing something to make a dent in the problems of this world and shifting our culture toward something better and brighter.

So get out there, don't be too hard on yourself, and accept the fact that you'll never fully know what you're doing. You just have to keep chugging along anyway and trying the best you can. I know that's a weird way to end a book that is supposed to be The Ultimate Guide to Being a Young Activist, but the truth is, no changemaker ever, no youth activist *ever*, has fully known what they were doing. They just learned the best they could, did the best they could with the best intentions, and made the most change they could with what tools they had available to them. So what are you waiting for? The world is yours. Go make some productive noise, make some changes, and learn by jumping in headfirst and doing the work that needs to be done.

That's what I'm doing. That's what you have to do. That's all we can do. It's time to *be* Youth to Power, by speaking Truth to Power.

ACKNOWLEDGMENTS

First things first: thank-you to my parents for bringing me into this world and never clipping my wings. I would not be where I am today if my parents didn't trust me and give me the freedom to explore and do the work I needed to do, even though it meant spending less and less time with them. *Gracias, Mama, por siempre apoyarme, por traerme comida cuando estoy trabajando, y por tener paciencia conmigo en todo lo que hago.* Thank you, Dad, for always being my number one fan and typing up on our big, clunky computer the stories I dictated to you back when I was six and decided I was going to be a published author. Your support means the world to me, and it's so comforting to know that even when I'm hard on myself and believe I am not enough, you see that I am. *Gracias a mi Abuelita Lucila, Tía Stella, Tío Ellery, primas Ilana y Samantha, Tía Nora, Tío Hugo, Tío Henry, y toda mi familia en Colombia por su amor y apoyo constante. Nada me hace más feliz que hacerlos orgullosos.*

Thank you to my very first writing mentor, Kathryn Mora, for listening to the thirteen-year-old girl who told you that she wanted to be an author. Thank you for taking me seriously and not discrediting me because of my age—our email conversations about writing, literature, and publishing really helped me grow as a writer. In all our conversations about writing and beyond, you treated me as your equal. Being your writer pen pal has been amazing.

Thank you to Brian Klems for being the first person to officially publish my writing. It was an honor to be thirteen and writing for *Writers Digest*. I appreciate you considering my work with the same seriousness with which you considered that of adults who submitted to be published. Also, thank you to every single editor I've worked with since then, from the team at *The New York Times* to *The Guardian*. Thank you for publishing my op-eds and essays and giving my writing a platform to be heard by the world.

Thank-you to the lovely team at Hachette and my editors, Miriam and Mollie, for seeing the revolutionary potential in this book and helping me craft it into a masterpiece. Thank-you to the whole marketing and promotional team—without you, the word would not get out to folks who need the information within these pages. To the whole Hachette team, your belief in *Youth to Power* has carried this book to completion.

A very special thank-you to my activism family. Thank-you to my adult mentors at Zero Hour, Kimberly Benson, Mary Heglar, Shravya Jain, Sebi Medina Tayac, Jair Carrasco, Laura Sanders, Mrinalini Chakraborty, and of course my future campaign manager Natalie Mebane for giving me the wisdom and knowledge about organizing and activism that I have the privilege of passing on to the next generation of activists with this book. A very special shout-out to Natalie: Your relentless selfless support of me and Zero Hour has carried the movement so far. Without our phone calls that last for hours and you dropping wisdom bombs left and right and talking me through the most difficult situations,

Acknowledgments

I would not have been able to get through the past few years. Our presidential campaign team is going to be unstoppable.

Thank-you to the original Zero Hour squad, Nadia Nazar, Madelaine Tew, and Zanagee Artis for taking the plunge with me when I first floated the crazy idea of starting a youth climate movement from nothing. You are the reason Zero Hour has been able to accomplish so much, and it is an honor to fight for climate justice alongside you.

Thank-you so much to the whole team at Zero Hour (naming you all would take forever but believe me when I say I love you all to death) for your dedication to the movement, your sacrifice, your hard work, your talent, and your never-ending love and support. Building a movement with you has been the best thing I have ever done in my life, and it was only from going through heaven and hell with you all that I gained the knowledge that I needed to write this.

Thank-you to Tokata Iron Eyes, Jasilyn Charger, Alethea Phillips, Nina Rose, and all of the amazing indigenous youth for your work fighting to protect our mother earth. Thank you for being there for me when things get rough. You are my heroes, and this book (and my whole activist journey) would not have been possible without you laying the groundwork for me and all of the examples you set for me.

Thank-you to Sue Lenander, Helaina Piper, Michael Foster, Bogdana Manole, and all of the Seattle organizers who welcomed me into the activist world when I was a confused little freshman with no clue what I was getting myself into. And thank-you so much to the team at Our Children's Trust, who helped elevate me to live out the spirit of *Youth To Power* by helping me sue my state government. To Andrea Rodgers and the whole Our Children's Trust legal team, I am eternally grateful for the opportunity to hold power accountable.

And of course, thank-you to all of my teachers who have been so supportive and patient with me throughout this whole increasingly overwhelming process. Thank-you to all my kindergarten through sixth-grade teachers at West Seattle Montessori School who created an environment of creativity and open learning where I could be free to explore and be myself. Thank-you to all the seventh- and eighth-grade teachers at the Westside School, especially Susannah Muench, who created wonderfully unorthodox courses, activities, and classes where I was allowed to hone my creativity and critical thinking and empowered to take on the world. You gave me the unlimited knowledge of George Orwell and how history repeats itself that made it so even four years of Catholic high school could not wear away my determination to stand up to authority. (I'm kidding! Catholic high school, you were so much better than I thought you would be.) Seriously though, thank-you so much to Holy Names Academy and all of my ninth- through twelfth-grade teachers who put up with me being *that* activist kid in the class with my crazy activist schedule that caused me to miss so much school it was like I didn't even go there. Thank-you to head of the attendance office, Sister Linda Riggers, for showing me unwavering support for all of my climate justice work and for allowing me to miss literally months of school a year so I could do that work. Thank-you as well to Mrs. Little, Mrs. Dawson, and the rest of the administration for being so supportive and patient with me as I tried my very best to navigate both being present in high school and in my attempts to change the world. Thank-you to the whole faculty and staff of Holy Names for never holding me back.

And of course, thank-you to all my weirdo friends at Holy Names, especially Kendall and Olivia, who never fail to make me laugh and were there for me in every up-and-down moment our high school years threw at us. There's really nothing quite like

Acknowledgments

being a queer Jewish kid at an all-girls Catholic high school. It's so funny that of all places, Holy Names Academy is where I came out, found my queer chosen family, and became comfortable in my own skin. Queer kids at HNA (you know who you are), I don't think I would have made it out of being a high school activist alive (or out of the closet alive) without your unwavering support and our never-ending sarcastic, witty banter, and inside jokes so obscure they sound like another language to anyone around us.

Finally, thank-you to every single organizer and activist, young and old that I've met along my journey. You all have inspired the advice and lessons in this book in some small way. Your stories, drive, enthusiasm, and ideas give me the energy and hope to keep doing this work even when it gets difficult.

And to everyone I will meet in the journey of promoting this book, to everyone who will impact me and share their stories and inspire me further—a special thank you in advance.

BIBLIOGRAPHY

King, Martin Luther, Jr. "Letter from a Birmingham Jail." *Christian Century,* June 12, 1963. https://www.christiancentury.org/article/first-person/letter-birmingham-jail.

Manolis, Sophia. "What Does It Mean to Be an Activist?" *Southerner,* March 10, 2019. https://www.shsoutherner.net/opinion/2019/03/10/what-does-it-mean-to-be-an-activist/.

National Association for the Advancement of Colored People (NAACP). Criminal Justice Fact Sheet. NAACP. https://www.naacp.org/criminal-justice-fact-sheet/.

Southwest Network for Environmental and Economic Justice. *The Jemez Principles of Democratic Organizing.* Principles adopted at the meeting of the Environmental Justice Network, Jemez, New Mexico, December 6–8, 1996. https://www.ejnet.org/ej/jemez.pdf.

United Nations. *Nature's Dangerous Decline "Unprecedented": Species Extinction Rates "Accelerating."* United Nations Sustainable Development Goals (blog). https://www.un.org/sustainabledevelopment/blog/2019/05/nature-decline-unprecedented-report/.

"Writing Effective Op-Eds." Duke University Communicator Toolkit. https://commskit.duke.edu/writing-media/writing-effective-op-eds/.

INDEX

Index

Index

Index

Index

Index

Index

Index

Index

Index

Index

Index

Index

Index

Index

Index

Index

ABOUT THE AUTHOR

Jamie is an eighteen-year-old Colombian American community organizer, activist, author, and public speaker. In her freshman year of high school, she was the youngest intern at her local campaign office and after election season was over, she joined grassroots groups in her community. She co-founded an international youth climate justice organization, Zero Hour, leading official "Youth Climate Marches" in Washington, DC and 25+ cities globally during the summer of 2018. These Zero Hour marches helped inspire and lay the groundwork for Greta Thunberg and the School Strike for Climate/Fridays for Future movement. Zero Hour has been at the forefront of organizing the mass school strike actions, and also organizes summits, educational campaigns, tours, workshops, and community events for climate action.

While in high school, Jamie organized countless mass mobilizations for change, revolutionary events, wrote op-eds for major publications such as *The New York Times, TIME Magazine,* CNN, and *The Guardian*, and traveled on multiple USA and international speaking tours. Jamie is also a plaintiff on *Our Children's Trusts' Youth v. Gov Washington* state lawsuit, suing Washington for denying her generation's constitutional right to a livable environment.

Jamie is one of *Teen Vogue's* 21 under 21 young women changing the world, *Fuse* TV's Latina Trailblazer of 2018, BBC's 100 most influential women of 2019, one of *People Magazine's* 25 women shaping the world, winner of an MTV EMA award in 2019 for her activism, one of *Forward's* 50 most influential Jews of 2019, one of *17 Magazine's* voices of 2019, and Telemundo's most influential women of 2019.